Cambridge Elements

Elements in Christian Doctrine
edited by
Rachel Muers
University of Edinburgh
Ashley Cocksworth
University of Roehampton
Simeon Zahl
University of Cambridge

THE *IMAGO DEI*

A Holistic Account

Ximian Xu
University of Cambridge

Shaftesbury Road, Cambridge CB2 8EA, United Kingdom

One Liberty Plaza, 20th Floor, New York, NY 10006, USA

477 Williamstown Road, Port Melbourne, VIC 3207, Australia

314–321, 3rd Floor, Plot 3, Splendor Forum, Jasola District Centre,
New Delhi – 110025, India

Cambridge University Press is part of Cambridge University Press & Assessment,
a department of the University of Cambridge.

We share the University's mission to contribute to society through the pursuit of
education, learning and research at the highest international levels of excellence.

www.cambridge.org
Information on this title: www.cambridge.org/9781009642521

DOI: 10.1017/9781009642569

© Ximian Xu 2026

This publication is in copyright. Subject to statutory exception and to the provisions
of relevant collective licensing agreements, no reproduction of any part may take
place without the written permission of Cambridge University Press & Assessment.

When citing this work, please include a reference to the DOI 10.1017/9781009642569

First published 2026

A catalogue record for this publication is available from the British Library

ISBN 978-1-009-64252-1 Hardback
ISBN 978-1-009-64255-2 Paperback
ISSN 2977-0211 (online)
ISSN 2977-0203 (print)

Cambridge University Press & Assessment has no responsibility for the persistence
or accuracy of URLs for external or third-party internet websites referred to in this
publication and does not guarantee that any content on such websites is, or will remain,
accurate or appropriate.

For EU product safety concerns, contact us at Calle de José Abascal, 56, 1°, 28003
Madrid, Spain, or email eugpsr@cambridge.org

The *Imago Dei*

A Holistic Account

Elements in Christian Doctrine

DOI: 10.1017/9781009642569
First published online: February 2026

Ximian Xu
University of Cambridge
Author for correspondence: Ximian Xu, sx279@cam.ac.uk

Abstract: What does it mean to say that the human being is the *imago Dei*? This Element leverages the Reformed thinking of archetype-ectype to constructively develop a holistic account of the *imago*. That is, the image of God refers to *both* the signifier of God-human stories and the stories of ethical performances towards others *and* the motivator within the psychosomatic human person for the narration of these stories that have been unfolding since Genesis 2. Furthermore, this Element will argue that the religious and ethical implications of the *imago Dei* are not confined to the contexts of the Christian faith but bear upon the quotidian lives of all humankind, including atheists. To illustrate this, neuroscience and empathic AI will serve as two case studies, demonstrating how the psychosomatic human person as the *imago Dei* bears the unique role in the narration of both religious and ethical stories.

Keywords: Christian theology, science and religion, AI ethics, anthropology, Christian ethics

© Ximian Xu 2026

ISBNs: 9781009642521 (HB), 9781009642552 (PB), 9781009642569 (OC)
ISSNs: 2977-0211 (online), 2977-0203 (print)

Contents

1 The *Imago Dei* as the Basis of Christian Anthropology   1

2 The Conventional Interpretations of the *Imago Dei*   5

3 A Holistic Interpretation of the *Imago Dei*: Signifier and Motivator in Human Psychosomatic Wholeness   22

4 The *Imago Dei* in Science-Engaged Theology   41

5 Conclusion   57

   References   60

1 The *Imago Dei* as the Basis of Christian Anthropology

> The purpose of a Christian anthropology is twofold: by pointing the believer to his original creation in the image of God to produce gratitude, and by pointing him to his present miserable condition to produce humility.
>
> T. F. Torrance (2001, 13)[1]

This Element is dedicated to achieving the first purpose, while remaining mindful of the second, through constructive exploration of a holistic interpretation of the *imago Dei*. With the advancement of science and technology, both gratitude and humility often fade away from discourses on the meaning of being human. Biomedical technology is expected by some trans/post-humanists to enhance current human conditions such that humans can be liberated from biological limitations. Digital technology is commended as a means to recast human existence in the virtual world. Humans are keen on sketching their own image but, on many occasions, fail to reflect on the underlying question of the human being *in se*. This explains variegated caricatures of humanity and drives us to dig into how Christian theology can contribute to contemporary narratives of the human being. The purpose of this Element is to spell out how a holistic interpretation of the *imago Dei* can pave a way to account for the meaning of being human with gratitude as well as humility while responding to questions posed by atheism and technoscience.

The image (*ṣelem*) of God or *imago Dei* is a sparsely used term in the Bible. There are only two direct references to the *imago Dei* (Gen. 1:27; 9:6) in the Hebrew Bible. In Genesis 5:1, humans are described as created in the likeness (*demût*) of God; in Genesis 5:3, *ṣelem* refers to the image of Adam rather than the *imago Dei*. Some theologians like John Calvin (2011, 1.15.3) argue that the two Hebrew words *ṣelem* and *demût* are interchangeable without material conceptual distinction. By contrast, others like Thomas Aquinas register that 'image' should be distinguished from 'likeness' in a nuanced way, defining likeness as '[the] perfection of the image' (Aquinas 2012, I, q.93, art.9, resp). Despite the divergence between the construals of likeness, most attention has been drawn to the conceptual and theological clarification on 'image'. This constant theological interest in the *imago Dei* may be largely rooted in the consistent focus on the New Testament accounts of the image (εἰκών) of God (1 Cor. 11:7; 2 Cor. 3:18; Col. 3:10) and, particularly, on Christ as the true image of God (2 Cor. 4:4; Col. 1:15).[2]

---

[1] Torrance makes this statement based on John Calvin's theological anthropology (Calvin 2011, 1.15.1).

[2] Heb. 1:3 employs χαρακτήρ to refer to Jesus Christ as 'the exact imprint of God's very being' (NRSV). An insightful reflection on this verse in relation to the image of God, see Kelsey 2009, 2:967–988. Jas. 3:9 describes humanity as created in the likeness (ὁμοίωσις) of God.

The *imago Dei* did not garner as much theological attention as Christology and the doctrine of the Trinity in the early Church. Apologists and church fathers took pains to pursue Christian orthodoxy while tackling theological issues and challenges related to the doctrine of the Trinity and Christology. It stands to reason that the creeds of the early Church do not reserve space to articulate the theological meaning of being human, let alone to speak of the *imago Dei*. That said, church fathers – such as Irenaeus of Lyons, Gregory Nazianzen, and Augustine – have offered varied accounts of the *imago Dei*, which cannot be reductively epitomised by a mere preoccupation with the rational faculty. (I will revisit this matter in Subsection 2.1.) Medieval theologians such as Bonaventure and Aquinas also presented rich reflections on the relevance between the *imago Dei* and humanity with an emphasis on the soul and reason. (It is misleading to argue that medieval theologians simply equate the *imago Dei* with the human soul or reason. We will return to this subject later.) Whilst attending to human substance and nature, Reformation theologians and their followers linked the *imago Dei* with their theological principle of human depravity and salvation by grace alone, leading to a methodology that consistently construes the *imago Dei* with an emphasis on soteriology.[3] By doing so, they deliberately warded off any tendency to affirm a postlapsarian human capacity for communion with God. Although ṣelem and εἰκών are rarely used in the Bible, the image of God has become a key concept in theological debate. To borrow John Paul II's words, the *imago Dei* 'constitutes the immutable basis of all Christian anthropology' (Paul 1988, III.6).

The discussion surrounding the *imago Dei* continued to flourish throughout the modern era and into the present century, and this theological theme has been tethered to human uniqueness and dignity. However, theological anthropology should confront challenges emerging in the wake of Enlightenment Newtonian natural philosophy and the modern sciences – which are, according to John Slattery, defined as 'the accepted scholarly study of natural things' (Slattery 2020, 2).[4] Newtonian natural philosophy recast Isaac Newton's theory raised in *Philosophiæ Naturalis Principia Mathematica* to naturalise the world as a machine without reference to God and religion.[5] If the human being is a part of nature as a machine, then the religious and transcendental implications of the *imago Dei* are highly vulnerable to doubt. A typical example is Julien Offray de

---

[3] On the *imago Dei* in the Lutheran and the Reformed theological anthropologies, see, e.g., Berkouwer 1962, 46–48; Heppe 2007, 220–250.

[4] This broad definition enables Slattery to classify industrial science and technology, education, and language science as branches of modern science.

[5] See further Shank 2019, 77–96.

la Mettrie's *Machine Man* (1747), which denies the need for an immaterial soul and describes the human being as an automaton (De La Mettrie 1996, 1–40).

The thriving of the modern sciences such as biological evolution, quantum physics, and Big Bang cosmology triggered the decline of the Enlightenment Newtonian worldview and gave birth to a dynamic one. The modern sciences reshape the interpretation of the *imago Dei* in an interdisciplinary way and – as will be unpacked – dispute some conventional understandings of the human being as the image-bearer. By way of brief illustration, evolutionary theory indicates the continuity and kinship between *Homo sapiens* and other animals, eliciting reconsideration of human uniqueness and its theological underpinning – the *imago Dei*. How can the image of God be understood in an inclusive sense so that humans and other animals belong in the same community? Recent rapid advancement of digital technology also poses challenges to the received construal of the *imago Dei*. For example, having examined humanoid robots, Anne Foerst (1998, 91–111) suggests that the *imago Dei* as promise and performance to *create* relationships does not qualitatively distinguish human beings from animals or machines insofar as humanoid robots mirror humanity and display both God-given creative powers and imagination. In this way, humanoid robots can be assimilated into human communities and contribute to the flourishing of human life.

With the various accounts of and challenges to both the concept of the *imago Dei* and its associated anthropological questions in mind, this Element aims to constructively articulate the *imago Dei* through engagement with recent interpretations of this Christian anthropological theme. As such, it will not engage with debates over the emergence of the *imago Dei*, which is often related to evolutionary theory.[6] Rather, it proceeds from the theological premise that the human being was created in the *imago Dei*, exploring the meaning and implications of the image instead of its emergence. It will argue that the *imago Dei* primarily means *both* the signifier of God-human stories and the stories of ethical performances towards others *and* the motivator created within humanity for the narration of these stories. It is the psychosomatic human person that participates in the narration of these stories, which have been unfolding since Genesis 2 and persist throughout the history of humanity. As such, the religious and ethical implications of the *imago Dei* extend beyond the context of the Christian faith and bear on the quotidian lives of all humankind, including atheists.

---

[6] On the debates over the emergence of the *imago Dei* in reference to human evolution, see, e.g., Berry 2012, 12–38; Deane-Drummond 2012, 39–46 (a response to Berry's position); De Smedt and De Cruz 2014, 135–156.

This Element will proceed to substantiate this thesis over the course of three sections. In Section 2, I will examine the four conventional interpretations of the *imago Dei*. The *imago Dei* is often viewed as either human reason or soul, or human stewardship delegated by God for exercising dominion on earth, or human relationships with others, or something to be fulfilled at the eschaton. It will be demonstrated that none of these interpretations fully captures the meaning and depth of the *imago Dei* insofar as they each fail to spell out the holistic implications of being human conveyed by the image of God. The human being exists as a *psychosomatic* unity in here-and-now *communities* while remaining oriented towards the future. Therefore, the *imago Dei* ontologically underpins individual human existence and the community of humankind, and endures throughout the history of humanity.

Section 3 will look into how the Reformed theology of archetype-ectype has been used to articulate a holistic understanding of humanity and how this pair of theological notions should be further investigated in tandem with the theological theme of the *imago Dei*. It will be made clear that the thinking of archetype-ectype offers an ontological framework for understanding the *imago Dei* in terms of psychosomatic humanity, which in turn paves a way for a holistic account of the *imago Dei* for both individuals and communities. That is, the *imago Dei* signifies God-human stories and the stories of ethical performances towards others, and serves as the motivator within humanity to dispose humans to narrate these stories. Attention will be given to how the holistic interpretation of the *imago Dei* responds to atheism, arguing that atheists also narrate these stories in their own way. In this light, the implications of the *imago Dei* reach beyond Christian communities and pertain to all of humanity.

In Section 4, I will leverage the corollaries drawn in Section 3 to probe how the psychosomatic human person created in the *imago Dei* narrates religious and ethical stories. The rationale of science-engaged theology will come into play here, which suggests that sciences as a type of experience serve as a source for theological reflection. Following this, artificial intelligence (AI) and neuroscience will be employed to develop two case studies on the respective narration of religious and ethical stories. First, I will illustrate that neuroscience is conducive to revealing how the *imago Dei* as the motivator and the signifier enables the psychosomatic human person to narrate God-human stories. Emphasis will fall on neurotheology, demonstrating the human person's biological capacity to sense the divine. The second part of this section will be devoted to showcasing the ethical significance of the *imago Dei* in relation to AI, with a focus on ethical issues related to empathy and human–AI interaction. I will enquire into the way in which the *imago Dei* furnishes an ethical tool for imaging empathy in AI systems by augmenting human empathic actions towards others. As such, rather than acting as a substitute for human beings, AI extends the human narration of ethical performances towards others.

These three sections together will elucidate how the holistic account of the *imago Dei* articulated in this Element will advance interdisciplinary research on psychosomatic humanity. Furthermore, it will come to be seen that the holistic interpretation possesses significant potential to deepen and broaden theological engagement with the meaning of being human and its associated ethical significance, which is expected to foster and consolidate a cross-cultural approach to anthropology. I am now proceeding to examine the conventional interpretations of the *imago Dei*.

2 The Conventional Interpretations of the *Imago Dei*

The *imago Dei* has been construed in varying senses, each placing emphasis on particular aspects of humanity and indicating a specific meaning of being human. The various conceptions of the *imago Dei* can be organised into four hermeneutical frameworks: the substantive, the functional, the relational, and the eschatological. The substantive framework is also named the structural interpretation of the *imago Dei*. It identifies the *imago Dei* with a specific component, characteristic, or capacity intrinsic to humanity. Unlike the substantive one, the functional framework avoids seeking a specific object and homes in on the performance of humans, defining the *imago Dei* as the God-given stewardship that humans assume to achieve certain tasks. Instead of concentrating upon humans themselves, the relational framework links the *imago Dei* to one's relationship with others and positions human relationality as the locus of significance within the being of humans. The eschatological framework looks to what will be given to humans in the future, which is often envisioned from the Christological perspective and thereby highlights the new humanity in Jesus Christ. By doing so, it more often than not makes the *imago Dei* abstract or lacks explanatory strength when fleshed out within the non-Christian spheres of the created order.

The four frameworks do not compete against one another. Some interpretations of the *imago Dei* can be situated within more than one framework. Notwithstanding that the four frameworks have brought forth a diverse range of hermeneutical insights into the *imago Dei*, they do not capture the full sense of the *imago Dei* with a holistic principle of the collective nature of humanity *and* the psychosomatic unity of the human being, which is derived from the religious and ethical implications of the *imago*. In this section, I will critically analyse the four hermeneutical frameworks and explore the aspects that merit a holistic understanding of the *imago Dei*.

2.1 The Substantive or Structural Framework

Having identified the *imago Dei* with human reason, the rational faculty, intellectual capability, or the soul, the substantive or structural framework is often traced back to church fathers and has developed over centuries of reflection on Christian anthropology. The bishop of Hippo is repeatedly drawn in support. Augustine's exegesis of Genesis 1:26–27 suggests that the creation of humankind after the *imago Dei* connotes the intellectual and rational faculties, which lie in the human soul (Augustine 2002, 3.20.30–32; 10.2.3). As such, he argues that 'each individual man who is not called the image of God according to everything that pertains to his nature, but according to the mind alone, is one person and is the image of the Trinity in his mind' (Augustine 1963, 15.7.11). In like manner, Gregory Nazianzen is invoked as a patristic source of the substantive framework. He asserts that the soul is created in the image of God such that humans are capable of imitating God (Gregory 2003, 6.14; also see 1894, 28.17). As God's image, humans come from and return to God, 'tam[ing] the flesh by the spirit' with Christ as their guide (Gregory 2001, 158).

That said, it is an overly reductive way to derive a corollary that both Augustine and Gregory Nazianzen represent a preliminary substantive framework for the interpretation of the *imago Dei*. The sophistication of patristic theology must be borne in mind when delving into their concepts of *imago Dei*. Augustine's identification of the *imago Dei* with the rational mind should be understood in his theological spectrum of reason. Integral to his position is the concurrence of reason, faith, and love, which are created to operate together to direct the human being to God for wisdom and eternal happiness (Augustine 1963, 10.5.7; 14.14.18; 14.19.26). Following this line of thought, the rational mind as the locus of the *imago Dei* is, in Augustine's work, taken to signify the spiritual communion between God and humans, which is to unfold throughout the journey of human life. By the same token, Gregory's theology of the *imago Dei* should be unravelled in respect of his broader theological themes. Recent studies on Gregory's theology demonstrate that he conceptualises the *imago Dei* in relation to the whole human person in order to bring to light the potential that humans possess for *theosis* (Thomas 2019). Indeed, both Augustine's and Gregory's concepts of the *imago Dei* are characterised by an emphasis on human rationality. This tendency, however, cannot be reduced to a simple equation of the *imago Dei* with the soul or the rational mind.

Such oversimplified hermeneutical approaches to Augustine's and Gregory's works are also evident in studies on Thomas Aquinas's theology of the *imago Dei*. These studies share the point of view that the *imago* is primarily defined by

Aquinas as the soul and rational mind (e.g., Emery 2007; Pasnau 2004).[7] Few studies attribute to Aquinas a conception of the *imago Dei* that theoretically incorporates human bodies. It should be conceded that Aquinas gives precedence to the soul and mind over the body, arguing that the mind alone is the image of God (Aquinas 2012, I, q.93, art.6, s.c.). He even goes so far as to claim that angels are a better image of God in their intellectual nature insofar as they are not attached to physical bodies (Aquinas 2012, I, q.93, art.3, resp). Be that as it may, Aquinas contends that the full sense of the *imago Dei* cannot be presented without reference to the body.

> Although the image of God in man is not to be found in his bodily shape, yet because *the body of man alone among terrestrial animals is not inclined prone to the ground, but is adapted to look upward to heaven, for this reason we may rightly say that it is made to God's image and likeness*.... But this is not to be understood as though the image of God were in man's body; but in the sense that the very shape of the human body represents the image of God in the soul by way of a trace. (Aquinas 2012, I, q.93, art.6, ad.3)

Aquinas makes it clear that a comprehensive interpretation of the *imago Dei* pertains to both the soul and the body, which together indicate the heavenly oriented human life, that is, the human journey towards God himself. His view of the *imago Dei*, in a broad sense, belongs to the substantive framework, provided that the structural understanding encompasses the significance of the physical body for the *imago Dei*. This position has found resonance in the work of other theologians. For example, John Calvin registers that the glory of the *imago Dei* shines through bodies while the soul is the primary seat of the image (Calvin 2011, 1.15.3). Both Aquinas and Calvin would turn down the suggestion that the soul alone can fathom the meaning of the *imago*.

That being so, the substantive framework involves more than the simplified identification between the *imago Dei* and the soul or the rational mind. It extends across every part of the human being, albeit prioritising the role of the soul and the rational mind. Taking this in account, it is an invalid criticism that the substantive framework turns out to denigrate human bodies, as Van Huyssteen (2006, 134) contests. Furthermore, the substantive understanding associates the human journey towards God with the *imago Dei*. The soul and the rational mind are not determinative of the meaning of the *imago Dei*. Rather, being the *imago Dei* is predicated upon human spiritual communion with God, which is constantly operative in the human journey towards the divinely given destiny and in which the rational mind plays a crucial role.

---

[7] It is argued that the structural framework was developed in the early church and extended through the medieval church (Cortez 2010, 18).

Having reconsidered the substantive framework, it suffices to contend that certain arguments levelled against this framework lack analytical rigour and are theoretically tenuous. One illustrative concern is about the connection between humans and other creatures. To locate the *imago Dei* in the soul is supposed to deny commonalities shared between humans and the rest of creation, which have been confirmed by the scientific discoveries of biological evolution (Cortez 2010, 19–20). Nevertheless, the due place of the human physical body within the substantive framework signifies the affinity between humans and other creatures, as they were alike formed out of the ground (Gen. 2:19). A second concern pertains to the exemplification of the *imago Dei* among those whose rational capacity is impaired or premature (Crisp 2015, 218–219). The human journey towards God offers a top-down theological apparatus through which to expand the substantive framework to comprise the whole human person with the soul as the start point of the journey. The purpose of the substantive interpretation of the *imago Dei* is not to demonstrate human rationality. In fact, the impaired or premature rational faculty does not rule out the human being's potential for living towards God.

Contrary to these critiques, a recent robust defence of the substantive framework is offered by Aku Visala's theory of property dualism. For Visala, a major distinction should be made between property and substance dualism: 'Property dualists think that only physical substances exist but that some properties that these substances have are more or less nonphysical. Against this, substance dualists believe that in addition to physical substances there are nonphysical substances' (Visala 2018, 69; also see 2014, 105; 2015b, 67–68). While substance dualism puts the body alongside the soul as two substances, property dualism treats the soul and the rational mind as nonphysical properties of the human substance. 'Physical' is not the antonym of 'nonphysical' in terms of property dualism. On the contrary, the physical and the nonphysical belong together in the human being with the former as the origin of the latter. In this way, both physical bodies and nonphysical properties, such as the soul, the rational mind, and reason, are equally valued.

Having foregrounded property dualism, Visala leverages evolutionary theory to reformulate the structural interpretation of the *imago Dei*.

> Dualists readily admit that souls are emergent and depend on the function of the body and the brain. When bodies and brains evolve, various capacities emerge and get shaped by the environment. What souls add to the mix is the existence of the person: self-consciousness where the outputs of cognitive systems come together. [The structural theology of the *imago Dei*] entails that there must be a point where the first human soul emerges – a point in time

before which there were no human souls (images of God) and after which there were human souls. (Visala 2018, 71–72)

With the emergence of the *imago Dei*, human uniqueness is affirmed – that is, human capacities 'to be addressed by God and to respond to him' (Visala 2018, 78; also see Visala and Fuentes 2015, 34). Visala's reconfigured structural interpretation clearly exhibits similarities to the aforementioned theologians like Augustine and Gregory Nazianzen. In contradistinction to them, Visala's property dualism safeguards the structural framework from portraying the soul and the body as two distinct substances, thereby circumventing the challenge of denigrating the physical body.

With that being said, Visala's structural theory of the *imago Dei* invites criticism. That is, it is a misreading of the relevant biblical texts that the *imago Dei* denotes the soul. Joel Green contends that 'the identification of the human soul with creation in God's image is alien to scripture and, in fact, should be abandoned' (Green 2015, 179). He looks closely at the phrase 'the breath of life' in the Genesis texts. In Genesis 2:7, the phrase does not imply that the soul was given to humans after their bodies were formed from the dust of the ground, because the same phrase is also employed to describe all life forms in Genesis 1:30 and 6:17. 'The breath of life' means nothing other than the fact that the life of all creatures comes from God (Green 2015, 181).[8] Following this, Green (2015, 185–188) maintains that the concept of the *imago Dei* as the soul is rooted in Platonism and Philo of Alexandria's philosophy, which is out of tune with the creation narratives in Genesis texts.

Green's argument challenges Visala's structural view of the *imago Dei* as well as the substantive framework in general. Prior to equating the *imago Dei* with a component, property, or capacity of human beings, the proponents of the substantive framework are urged to demonstrate how their understandings of the *imago Dei* fit in with the biblical narratives of creation. It is precisely at this point that the exponents of the functional framework claim greater analytical and explanatory rigour.

2.2 The Functional Framework

A widely received functional framework is to construe the *imago Dei* as the God-given regency to exercise dominion over the earth and all creation, which proceeds from the juxtaposition of 'image' and 'dominion' in Genesis 1:26–28. A consensus has been reached that the functional interpretation reflects the

---

[8] Noort Ed (2016, 1–15) suggests in a like manner that Genesis 2:7 does not present a dualistic picture of body and soul. 'The breath of life' simply means 'the intangible life force which animates the body' (9).

ancient Near Eastern and Mesopotamian background of Genesis. That is, ancient Near Eastern mythologies describe kings as divine representatives to exercise dominion over the world.[9] It is argued that the *imago Dei* somehow echoes these mythologies and thus reflects the kingly status of humankind.

In his commentary on Genesis, Gerhard von Rad's exegesis of these three verses, arguably, offers the most iconic functional interpretation of the image of God and sheds light on the relevant exegetical logic.

> The close relation of the term for God's image with that for the commission to exercise dominion emerges quite clearly when we have understood *selem* as a plastic image. Just as powerful earthly kings, to indicate their claim to dominion, erect an image of themselves in the provinces of their empire where they do not personally appear, so man is placed upon earth in God's image as God's sovereign emblem.... The decisive thing about man's similarity to God, therefore, is his function in the non-human world. (von Rad 1973, 59–60)

Von Rad makes it clear that the literary context of Genesis 1:26–28 delineates the conceptual boundaries of the *imago Dei*. Needless to say, this exegetical principle is acknowledged among those who hold the conviction that the Bible *per se* has already presented a clear and straightforward clarification on the meaning of the *imago Dei*.[10] A typical example is John Goldingay's exegesis of the Genesis texts related to the *imago Dei*. 'Being in the image of God,' he asserts, 'means that humanity rules over the earth' (Goldingay 2020, 45). Yet, the ruling neither signifies humanity's superiority to the animal world, nor suggests that human beings are granted with authority to exploit nature (Goldingay 2020, 45–46). On the contrary, the *imago Dei* indicates that human beings should exercise shepherdship over the world and bring forth harmony within creation (Goldingay 2020, 46).

Both von Rad and Goldingay articulate the functional interpretation of the *imago Dei* in light of biblical texts. Unlike them, others employ interdisciplinary approaches to elucidating the functional meaning of 'image.' Among such approaches, one innovative method is to unpack the functional significance of the *imago Dei* in tandem with evolutionary theory. Illustrative of this is Michael Burdett's integration of the *imago Dei* with human niche construction. A human niche refers to a sphere that ranges over human social, cultural, spatial, and

---

[9] For a detailed, in-depth analysis of the ancient cultural contexts of the image of God, see Herring 2013, particularly 25–48 and 87–127; Walton 2006, 212. Ronald Hendel in his recent commentary on Genesis (2024, 144–145) reminds us that Genesis sketches a cosmology distinct from that of the ancient Near East.

[10] 'Doubtless,' James Barr (1993, 158) argues, 'the most influential opinion today, however, is what ... the "functional" view: the image of God consists in human dominion over the world.' For a typical functional interpretation from a Jewish perspective, see Levenson 1988, 111–120.

ecological activities and contexts. Human niche construction (NC) means that humans live with other species through building, modifying, and reshaping the communal and shared environment. Burdett is convinced that the functional interpretation is conceptually closer to the Genesis texts than others insofar as both the functional understanding of the *imago Dei* and the NC theory 'valorize the agency of the organism in an environmental and social ecology that contributes to the flourishing and even transformation of the organisms in the niche' (Burdett 2020, 171). In other words, the significance of the function intrinsic to the image of God is unveiled through human agency to construct their niche. It is worth quoting Burdett's lengthy explication of the agency in terms of the image of God.

> The kind of agency associated with [the functional model of the *imago Dei*] and NC is about the directed shaping of a particular niche one presently inhabits. . ... What is more, this human agency on the environment has a divine mandate. The human being acts on the environment because (s)he acts as God's proxy and reflects the divine image within God's creation. That human agency arises out of a calling, an election or even a vocation to act on behalf of God for the sake of creation's providential development. Hence, NC activity within the framework of [the functional model of the *imago Dei*] unites the common faculty of human agency upon an environment, which is in continuity with other creatures that construct niches, with the divine calling of representative action in God's creation. (Burdett 2020, 172)

Accordingly, the *imago Dei* signals that humans are created to be God's partners in God's continuous providential work, contributing to the flourishing of creation. Being the *imago Dei* is to perform the agency of niche construction in transforming communal contexts for both humans and other species. While Burdett's interdisciplinary construal furnishes a more detailed treatment of the functional implication of the *imago Dei* than those found in von Rad and Goldingay, the three scholars all hold a common position that the functional understanding is primarily linked with the human being's relationship with creation and care for the created order.

The functional framework is slightly reframed in recent studies, turning away from the relationship between humanity and the rest of creation to God-human relationship. David Clines (1968, 82–83) registers that the image of God in the ancient East Asia carries the connotation of a spiritual union between kings and their deity. However, he does not expand upon the theological significance of the spiritual union.[11] In this regard, Richard Middleton's study recasts the functional interpretation of the *imago Dei* from a symbolic perspective.

---

[11] However, Clines (1968, 96) maintains that the human being's 'dominion over the animals cannot be definitive of the image' but 'virtually becomes a constitutive part of the image itself'.

Middleton (2005, 52) acknowledges that the Hebrew words *rādâ* (exercise dominion) and *kābaš* (subdue) in Genesis 1:26–29 do connote 'the human vocation with a distinctly royal hue' insofar as the growth of human community 'requires a significant exercise of communal power'. In his position, this royal hue does not ensure that the human dominion over the earth solely qualifies the *imago Dei* (Middleton 2005, 52–53). Connecting the *imago Dei* to the human dominion over the earth presupposes that God is depicted as the ruler in the creation narrative of Genesis 1 (Middleton 2005, 60–61; also see 70–74). Middleton turns down a superficial identification of God with ruler and suggests that Genesis 1 should be read within wider biblical contexts. Hence, he cites biblical passages across the Scripture to frame the literary context for understanding God's creation in Genesis 1.

Middleton maintains that the Genesis texts include multiple metaphors to characterise God's creation, including 'the metaphor of God as designer and artificer' (Middleton 2005, 74). God created, *designed*, and *built* the cosmos. With this in mind, the core question of the creation narrative of Genesis 1 is what building God designed and made through his creative activity according to his plan. Middleton asserts that 'the unequivocal answer given from the perspective of the rest of the Old Testament is this: God is building a *temple*' (Middleton 2005, 81; italics original).[12] Hence, Genesis 1 depicts God's creation of a cosmic sanctuary, supplementing what is missed in the royal hue associated with the *imago Dei*.

> But the *imago Dei* also includes a priestly or cultic dimension. In the cosmic sanctuary of God's world, humans have pride of place and supreme responsibility, not just as royal stewards and cultural shapers of the environment, but (taking seriously the temple imagery) as priests of creation, actively mediating divine blessing to the nonhuman world and – in a postfall situation – interceding on behalf of a groaning creation until that day when heaven and earth are redemptively transformed to fulfill God's purposes for justice and shalom. The human vocation as *imago Dei* in God's world thus corresponds in important respects to Israel's vocation as a 'royal priesthood' among the nations (Exodus 19:6). (Middleton 2005, 89–90)[13]

In Middleton's position, while the *imago Dei* implies the human dominion over the earth, the metaphor of the cosmos as the temple reveals that the human being's priestly agency to channel God's blessing into the rest of creation is the core value and function of being the *imago Dei*. To this extent, it can be argued

---

[12] Middleton (2005, 81) observes that the image of the temple accords with the ancient Near Eastern and Mesopotamian worldviews, which regard temples as the palaces of the gods. For further discussion of temples in ancient Near Eastern thought, see Walton 2006, 113–134.

[13] A similar position can be found in Blenkinsopp 2011, 25–29.

that Middleton's fine-tuning of the functional framework expands and enriches the responsibilities that God delegates to humans at creation.

The functional framework – which is widely endorsed in the area of biblical studies – has been disputed. The notable biblical scholar James Barr (1968, 11–26) asserts that the Genesis texts do not furnish a clear-cut concept of the *imago Dei*. That is to say, any attempt to make an affirmative definition of the *imago Dei* based on biblical texts turns out to be a-biblical. Added to Barr's contestation is an argument against the exegetical logic of the functional framework. Both the *imago Dei* as the human dominion over the earth and as the priestly agency to mediate God's grace share the commonality that their centre of gravity lies primarily in the Genesis texts and creation narrative. If the creation narratives of the Genesis texts are interpreted in light of broader biblical contexts as Middleton suggests, then the theological motif of Christ as the true image of God (2 Cor. 4:4; Col. 1:15) in the New Testament must be integrated into the functional implication of the *imago Dei*, which is, however, underexplored in Middleton's reconfigured functional framework. How does Christ as *the* image of God reveal human priestly agency? As will be unpacked, the Christological motif goes beyond the functional framework and contributes to a holistic interpretation of the *imago Dei*.

2.3 The Relational Framework

The *imago Dei* as relational means that the human person's relationship with others is inherent to the being of humans. *Contra* the functional framework that is rooted in the exegesis of the Genesis texts, the relational framework is predicated upon the theological reflection on the *imago Dei*, particularly under the auspices of the doctrine of the Trinity. The phrase 'let us make' in Genesis 1:26 is considered to imply the intra-Trinitarian communion, suggesting that the creation of humanity ultimately mirrors the relationship between the three divine persons. Associating the plural word 'us' with the Trinity can be traced back to the early church. For example, Irenaeus of Lyons (1885, 4.20.1) submits that the Father addresses 'Let us make' to the Son and the Spirit. However, that relationality is viewed as the core meaning of the *imago Dei* in light of the intra-Trinitarian communion did not gain prominence in Christian anthropology as well as dogmatics until the twentieth century. On this front, Karl Barth – who articulates the relational implication of the *imago Dei* through both Trinitarian and Christological lenses – made a substantial contribution to the formation and development of the relational framework.

Barth's concept of the *imago Dei* is grounded in his theocentric understanding of the being of humans, which maintains that humanity is ultimately *determined* by God, the divine Thou.

> Being with means encounter. Hence being with the other man means encounter with him. Hence humanity is the determination of our being as a being in encounter with the other man. . ... The basic formula to describe it must be as follows: 'I am as Thou art.' . . . It tells us that every 'I am' is qualified, marked and determined by the 'Thou art.' Owing it to God the Creator that I am, I am only as Thou art; as, created by the same God, Thou art with me. (Barth 2004, III.2, 247–248)[14]

Integral to Barth's position is the conviction that the understanding of humanity should be ultimately shaped by the knowledge of the divine being. 'Thou art' is always the ontological foundation of 'I am'. Barth reiterates in *Church Dogmatics* that God is not solidary but rather is in fellowship in himself (e.g., Barth 2004, I.1, 354; I.2, 34; II.1, 475–476; III.4, 103–104). The intra-Trinitarian communion determines 'I am'. The *Deus triunus* creates fellow-humanity rather than a *homo solitarius*, and this relationality inherent to humanity is the essence of the *imago Dei* and is determinative of the meaning of being human (Barth 2004, III.4, 117).[15]

Barth spells out the relational nature of the *imago Dei* in two respects.[16] First, the *imago Dei* refers to the identity of the human being as God's counterpart and covenant-partner. The creation of humanity in the *imago Dei* is God's inviting humans to participate in rest with him, which reveals God's covenant of grace (Barth 2004, III.1, 98). As such, Barth registers that the human being, who is determined by God as his counterpart, 'exists originally and properly in an inner connexion and correspondence between his divine determination and his creaturely form, between his being as the covenant-partner of God and his being as man' (Barth 2004, III.2, 135, 205). For this reason, the human being is created and, consequently, bears the responsibility to hear, understand, and respond to God's covenantal address (e.g., Barth 2004, III.2, 17–18, 126, 203). It is at this point that Barth locates Christology at the centre of his theology of the *imago Dei*. Jesus Christ as the true *imago Dei* is the true covenant-partner, in whose history the responsibility to respond to God's address is fulfilled (Barth 2004, III.2, 207–222). Given the Christological basis, the human *imago Dei* can be restored only in Jesus Christ, and the being of humans is solely known in him. The *imago Dei* is inextricably associated with the *imago Christi*.

The second aspect of the relational nature of the *imago Dei* is the fellowship between human persons, which is derived from their identity as God's

---

[14] For further analysis of Barth's view of the human being, see Jones 2019, 389–406.

[15] Barth (2004, III.1, 182–185) argues that the phrase 'let us make' signifies the creative work of the Triune God.

[16] Colin Gunton's formulation of the *imago Dei* follows Barth's line of thought; see Gunton 1991, 47–61.

covenant-partner. '[The human being's] ordination to be in covenant relation with God has its counterpart in the fact that his humanity, the special mode of his being, is by nature and essence a being in fellow-humanity' (Barth 2004, III.4, 116). In Barth's position, fellow-humanity is exemplified by the relationship between male and female, which is corresponding to the intra-Trinitarian relationship and is thus normative and foundational for other human–human relationships (Barth 2004, III.4, 117).

Barth's Trinitarian and Christological formulation of the *imago Dei* brings forth a revolutionary dogmatic treatment of this theological theme. Indeed, a number of arguments have been raised to challenge and dispute Barth's position. Wolfhart Pannenberg (1985, 59–60) argues that Barth's Trinitarian and Christological approach may make the *imago Dei* something external to the human being and solely pertinent to God himself, which seems to suggest that God's creation is not so effective as determining the entire dispositions, life, and existence of human beings. Jürgen Moltmann (1985, 215–225, 252–255) observes that Barth's view of the *imago Dei* and theological anthropology as a whole are characterised as spiritualisation, which turns out to be oblivious to human history and dynamic human becoming. Despite appreciating and appropriating Barth's relational interpretation of the *imago Dei*, Moltmann (1985, 234–243) articulates a concept of the *social imago Dei*, which qualifies the human community by *imago* and stresses the history of humans within their own communities as revealing the Trinitarian communion.

The relational hermeneutical framework has diffused across studies on theological anthropology. F. LeRon Shults's work on theological anthropology is a case in point. He expands upon the relational nature of the *imago Dei* mindful of the philosophical turn to relationality, which is dissatisfied with the privileging of substance and attends closely to the social, cultural, and physical aspects of humanity (Shults 2003, 2). For Shults, the relational nature of the *imago Dei* refers to how humans *glorify* God.

> Humans are created 'in' the image and 'after' the likeness of God because their very being as persons is oriented toward sharing in the wisdom of the One whose Spirit raised Christ from the dead (Rom. 8:11). Our imaging of God vis-a-vis our neighbors means precisely that (like Christ) we do not seek our own glory but lay down our lives (our ontological security) for the other in love. (Shults 2003, 241)

Shults (2003, 241–242) believes that the glory-oriented interpretation of the *imago De* helps ease human ontological anxiety and enables us to look to the future communion with God. This resonates with the eschatological interpretation of the *imago Dei*, which will be detailed next.

The relational interpretation of the *imago Dei* is recently deployed within interaction between theology and sciences. For example, Noreen Herzfeld (2002; also see 2012, 500–509) argues that the *imago Dei* signifies humanity's capacity to respond to God's address, which means that conversation is characteristic of the relational nature of humans and should also feature in AI as the *imago hominis*. Having relationality as its central feature and function, AI can be considered belonging to human communities provided that human–human relationship is not replaced by human–AI relationship. (I will revisit this subject in Subsection 4.2.) In this way, human relationality given through the *imago Dei* extends beyond human existence, showing the way AI as well as other technologies can be deployed for human flourishing.

While the relational framework has much to offer to Christian anthropology, it also raises questions that have generated some critical responses. First, it largely makes relationality determinative of the wholeness of the human person. The determination of relationality casts the embodied wholeness of humanity into doubt. Do the psychosomatic aspects of the human being have their own value independent of human relationality since human relationship with others is coupled with psychic activities and is embodied in physical contexts? Does God's relationship with humans logically precede or follow the human being as the *imago Dei*? There are reasons to question whether the human being *qua* the *imago Dei* can be recapitulated solely in relationality.

Second, the relational understanding of the *imago Dei* relies upon the Trinitarian understanding of Genesis 1:26–29, interpreting 'let us make' as referring to the creative action of the Father, the Son, and the Spirit. However, the Trinity is not unambiguous in these four verses. The word 'us' is not necessarily theologically tethered to the Triune God. Ronald Hendel's recent commentary on Genesis challenges such exegesis. He suggests that the plural form in 'let us make' is best understood as God and his divine entourage (Job 38:7; 1 Kgs 22:19; Dan 7:9-10; Isa 6:1-8). This accords with the ancient Near Eastern worldview, which describes the creation of humans 'as a result of decisions in the divine assembly (Hendel 2024, 129).

> Against this backdrop, the 'us' in God's speeches in Genesis 1–11 is best understood as referring to the divine assembly.... This explains why God announces his decree in a plural address but performs the action by himself – the others are there as the backdrop for his deliberation, but God alone has the authority and power to create. (Hendel 2024, 129)[17]

In light of Hendel's exegesis, God addresses the divine assembly, followed by the creation of humanity in his image and likeness. Although 'our image' and

---

[17] A similar interpretation can be found in Wenham 1987, 28.

'our likeness' in Genesis 1:26 can be understood to imply plurality within Godhead, the Trinitarian reflection on the Genesis texts seems to read more into the texts than the immediate context implies.

The exegetical principle of the relational framework is diametrically opposed to that of the functional framework. The functional framework concentrates upon Genesis 1-2 and extends its exegetical corollaries to other biblical passages concerning the image of God, whereas the relational framework leverages the doctrine of the Trinity as well as Christology – articulated out of the entire Bible – to flesh out the meaning of the *imago Dei*. The relational and the functional frameworks take the opposite exegetical logics, and the exegetical principle of the relational framework is applicable to the eschatological framework, to which we are now turning.

2.4 The Eschatological Framework

The eschatological framework suggests that the main significance of the *imago Dei* will not be fulfilled until *the* future. It is often intertwined with the relational framework. An example of this type is Moltmann's social *imago Dei*, which, as noted earlier, stresses human history and communities. Yet, human history is determined not by humans themselves but rather by the divine history. Moltmann (1985, 228–229) argues that 'as God's image human beings conform to the presence of the Creator in his creation, and as God's children they conform to the presence of God's grace; but when the glory of God itself enters creation, they will become like God, and transfigured into his appearance. The *imago per conformitatem gratiae* points beyond itself to the *imago per similitudinem gloriae*'. The sociality of the *imago Dei* will be entirely actualised in the consummate human fellowship with God at the eschaton. The full meaning of the *imago Dei* will not be displayed until the eschaton.

Wolfhart Pannenberg presents a sophisticated account of the eschatological construct of the *imago Dei*, which originates in the bond between creation and eschatology. The creation of humanity and creation in general alike have the same purpose to 'share in the life of God' (Pannenberg 1991, 136). However, the fellowship with of God cannot be consummated until the eschaton. For this reason, the destiny of all creation – which has laid down by God in the beginning – will be fulfilled in the eschatological future through the coming of God's kingdom as proclaimed by Jesus Christ and mediated through the incarnation. In this light, despite their distinct theological intricacies, creation and eschatology are united and belong together (Pannenberg 1991, 138–146).[18]

---

[18] The theological principle underlying Pannenberg's correlation of creation and eschatology is the unity of the Triune God's action *ad extra*: 'The creation, preservation, and rule of the world are

The unity of creation and eschatology is foundational for the *imago Dei*. Pannenberg (1991, 180) asserts that the human destiny of the fellowship with God through Jesus Christ 'is the subject of the doctrine of our creation in the image of God'. Having turned down the functional interpretation, he maintains that the *imago Dei* must be construed in Jesus Christ as the true *imago Dei* in that *the eschatological new human being* to be given to believers in the future is only revealed in Jesus Christ (Pannenberg 1991, 208, 219–220). The radical distinction between Christological *imago Dei* and the *imago Dei* of the Genesis texts consists in human creation *according to* or *in* the *imago Dei* instead of *being* the image of God (Pannenberg 1991, 215–216). Furthermore, Pannenberg (1991, 216–217, 230–231) dissents from the conceptual identification between 'image' and 'likeness' in the Genesis texts and contests that 'likeness' as theologically essential to 'image' points to the destiny and full actualisation of humanity, which is mediated through the incarnation and the fellowship of the divine and the human in Jesus Christ. The full meaning and destiny of the *imago Dei* is proleptic rather than extrapolating out of the past. The future-determining nature of the *imago Dei* yields both existential and moral implications for human life.[19]

> The point of likeness to God is fellowship with him. We must understand our present life, and especially our personality, in terms of this future destiny.. .. The destiny is not just an isolated one. Its aim is the incorporation of humanity into the kingdom of God. Thus the common destiny of fellowship with God underlies and governs human relations. Only in the relation to God, and therefore in terms of the eschatological future of our destiny, does our moral self-determination or ethical autonomy find a firm and solid basis. (Pannenberg 1991, 224; also see 227–229)

The destiny of the fellowship with God valorises communal life as essential to human life. As has been noted in the relational framework, the eschatological interpretation integrates the *imago Dei* with human communal existence. Furthermore, the destiny generates a moral impact that guides here-and-now life. That is to say, all human–human relations and human ethical performances towards others should take shape in the anticipated full actualisation of the *imago Dei*, namely, the eschatological fellowship with God, which has been modelled in Jesus Christ.

---

related aspects of the one divine act by which the three persons of the Trinity together bring forth the reality of the creaturely world that is distinct from God. In this regard we saw that the concept of creation relates to the overarching unity of the divine act, that the concept of preservation relates the existence of creatures to their beginning, and that the divine rule aims at the future consummation' (Pannenberg 1991, 139).

[19] For further on this, see Wong 2008, 13–57.

Pannenberg's eschatological formulation of the *imago Dei* is favourably received in Stanley Grenz's work on theological anthropology. The primary objective of Grenz's work is to deploy the theological theme of the *imago Dei* to develop a social-personalist concept of the self within the postmodern context (Grenz 2001, 14). He maintains that the *imago Dei* signals the growth of human beings towards the new humanity that will ultimately be fulfilled in Jesus Christ, the preeminent image of God (Grenz 2001, 203–264). Of most relevance here is his argument that the *telic* or eschatological nature of the *imago Dei* leads to a social or ecclesial self, which is made by God's eschatological action in his love (Grenz 2001, 304–331).[20] In this respect, Grenz takes a further step beyond Pannenberg in capitalising on the eschatological significance of the *imago Dei* to frame the construct of self-in-community as a way to reveal the new humanity.

Grenz's eschatological account of the *imago Dei* bears out the contribution that Christian anthropology can make to the recovery of the social self in the postmodern context. However, J. Wentzel Van Huyssteen's caution against the downside of the eschatological interpretation deserves attention. He notes that 'any overly intellectualized, abstract vision of the goal of human life endangers the scriptural emphasis on *the whole human being* as 'created in the image of God' (Van Huyssteen 2006, 142; emphasis added). The clash between the abstract vision (e.g., the eschatological new humanity) and the concept of the whole human being is nothing other than the undermining of 'the full reality of the embodied human condition' (Van Huyssteen 2006, 154). Indeed, one can hardly say that Grenz ignores the human embodiment as he spills much ink on the *imago Dei* in relation to sexuality and community. Be that as it may, the eschatologically determined feature of the *imago Dei* may cast embodied human lives into the shadow of the abstract new humanity.

David Kelsey levels criticism against Grenz from the perspective of the relationship between creation and eschatological consummation. The main question Kelsey (2009, 2:904) raises concerning Grenz's eschatological reading of the *imago Dei* is as follows: 'Can eschatological consummation be understood simply as the final actualization of the goal of creation without the consequence that the movement from beginning to end just *is* God's creative act and that only at the eschatological state is "creation" truly actual?' Kelsey (2009, 2:904) contends that Grenz's methodology results in absorbing creation into eschatological consummation.

While Kelsey's magnum opus *Eccentric Existence* is not intended to develop the eschatological hermeneutical framework for the *imago Dei*, he elaborates on

---

[20] As such, Grenz (2001, 331–336) defines 'the church as the prolepsis of the divine image'.

the eschatological aspect of the *imago Dei*, which is constitutive of the pillars of Christian anthropology. Kelsey meticulously crafts a Christocentric approach to understanding the *imago Dei*. He argues that Jesus Christ as the *imago Dei* governs human knowledge of God, 'God's ways of relating to all else including human beings in community,' and human response to God (Kelsey 2009, 2:911, 961; also see 2:909).[21] The Christocentric approach and the theological theme of the *imago Dei* can demonstrate the unity of the three interrelated, yet distinct, ways in which Triune God relates to all creatures: relating to us to create us, relating to us to draw us to eschatological consummation, and relating to us to reconcile us in our self-estrangement from God (Kelsey 2009, 1:5, 2:896).

The three ways in which God relates to humans are intertwined with two foundational principles. First, the three ways correspond, respectively, to the three Trinitarian formulas: the Father through the Son in the power of the Spirit, the Spirit sent by the Father with the Son, and the Son sent by the Father in the power of the Spirit. These Trinitarian formulas together reveal that the image of God should exhibit how the Triune God relates to humankind. Specifically, the *imago Dei* refers to 'what human beings are as imagers of the image of God – namely, finite living mysteries that image the triune living mystery' (Kelsey 2009, 2:1009; also see 2:1026). Second, the three ways have a special logical ordering. God relating to create does not depend on the other two divine relating to humans insofar as creation has its own value that cannot be assimilated into either eschatological consummation or reconciliation. God relating to draw us to eschatological consummation presupposes God relating to create, and they together serve as the *conditio* sine qua non of God relating to reconcile (Kelsey 2009, 1:456–457; 2:607–608). Yet, the three distinct ways converge in the incarnation. Creatureliness, eschatological consummation, and reconciliation belong together in Jesus Christ, exhibiting Triune God's work *ad extra* (Kelsey 2009, 2:609).

Taking these two foundational principles together, it comes to the fore that Kelsey situates the eschatological nature of the *imago Dei* within the Trinitarian-Christocentric structure of *opus Dei pro nobis*, which reveals who the human being is in terms of the particular way in which God relates to draw humans to eschatological consummation (Kelsey 2009, 2:954–956). Furthermore, the eschatological nature of the *imago Dei* is of great import for human life.

---

[21] Kelsey (2009, 2:938) argues that 'the principal anthropological significance of the notion of the *imago Dei* emerges, not from its role in Genesis 1:26–27, but from its role in christological contexts in the New Testament. The significance of the notion of "image of God" for theological anthropology emerges ... when the question asked of the phrase "image of God" is "Who is the 'image'?" rather than "What is the 'image'?" and when the answer is, "Jesus Christ"'.

> Given that Jesus, as the image of God, is the prototypical human creature, all other living human bodies may be said to flourish as images of the image of God insofar as the bodied acts that constitute their concrete existential hows are bodily enactments of practices of hope – that is, practices that are appropriate responses to the way in which the triune God relates to draw them to eschatological consummation. (Kelsey 2009, 2:1029)

In this respect, Kelsey escapes aforementioned van Huyssteen's criticism concerning the embodied human condition and stresses the bearing that the theme of the *imago Dei* has on the multi-layered aspects of human life. Humen embodied existence is interwoven with all spheres of human life, be it economic, political, cultural, or otherwise. The *imago Dei* as signifying human response to God's relating to draw us to eschatological consummation has a role to play in these spheres.

That said, Kelsey's eschatological account of the *imago Dei* as well as Christian anthropology is open to criticism that it seems to lack significance outside Christianity. While recognising the independent value of creation, Kelsey's Christocentric-eschatological interpretation throws up a question about the application of the theological theme of the *imago Dei* within non-Christian circles like atheists. Are atheists the image of God in the Christocentric-eschatological terms? Indeed, Kelsey (2009, 1:27, 80) makes it clear that the primary purpose of his *Eccentric Existence* is not to account for the apologetic logic of coming to belief but rather for the logic of Christian beliefs.[22] Nonetheless, an in-depth investigation is required to explore how the *imago Dei* may be operative in non-Christian spheres, which can strengthen Kelsey's emphasis on both the independence of creation from eschatological consummation and the significance of the *imago Dei* for quotidian human existence.

2.5 Concluding Remarks

I have thus far analysed the four hermeneutical frameworks for the understanding of the *imago Dei*, each having its own distinct theological emphases and rationales. As noted earlier, the four frameworks do not necessarily rival one another. It has been demonstrated in this section that there are multiple points of overlap among the four frameworks, even more so in the relationship between the relational and the eschatological ones. Hence, it is logically consistent to argue that these four frameworks can work together to sketch a big theological

---

[22] On the analysis of the methodology of Kelsey's Christian anthropology, see John Thiel 2011, 1–13.

picture of the *imago Dei*. Gijsbert van den Brink strikes a right note about the potential to concatenate the four frameworks.

> For we are special for theological reasons. That is: we are special because God has called us to be stewards of God's earthly creation, having endowed us with the capacity for responsible relationships with each other and with Godself, relationships which we need in order to take care of each other and of creation as a whole in a myriad of ways. Moreover, in order to live in these responsible relationships and to fulfill our tasks, God has given us some substantive character traits which are, if not unique in kind then at least unique in degree as compared to any other species in creation. (van den Brink 2011, 331)

Added to this observation is that humans are special because they belong into the hope-oriented community and are drawn to eschatological consummation. In short, human uniqueness becomes a theological principle to govern the integration of the four frameworks.[23]

The correlation of the four frameworks also suggests that the concept of the *imago Dei* may, by its nature, have a theological apparatus through which to string together various understandings of humanity as the *imago Dei*. None of the four frameworks will dominate in the construal of the concept, but they each convey a characteristic feature of the *imago Dei* and are constitutive of the fabric of Christian anthropology. What has come to the fore in this section is that the four frameworks, to varying degree, share the conviction that the *imago Dei* should involve both the body and the soul. Even if the substantive framework normally places emphasis on the soul, recent studies of this type – as noted earlier – have paid due attention to human psychosomatic unity as essential to the nature of humanity. As will be unpacked in the next section, it is the holistic account of the psychosomatic wholeness of the human being *both* that furnishes a hermeneutical tool to bring forth a fuller meaning of the *imago Dei* than the four frameworks, *and* that makes the *imago Dei* an anthropological theme not limited within Christian confines but operative within broader, general contexts.

3 A Holistic Interpretation of the *Imago Dei*: Signifier and Motivator in Human Psychosomatic Wholeness

The deeper significance of the *imago Dei* remains to be explored. For, if the *imago Dei* is concerned with who the human being is, then its implication should be relevant to and effective for both Christian communities in particular

---

[23] Arguments have been raised against the claim that the *imago Dei* indicates human uniqueness (e.g., Moritz 2011, 307–339; 2020, 537–551). On the contrary, others make compelling arguments with van den Brink that the *imago Dei* theologically underlies human uniqueness (e.g., Barrett and Greenway 2017, 64–81; Burdett 2015, 3–10; Polkinghorne 2010, 28–30).

and quotidian human life in general. This section is dedicated to digging out how the theological theme of humanity as the *imago Dei* can be conceptualised with an eye to shed light on the meaning of being humans in such a way that it is relevant across both Christian and non-Christian spheres. By doing so, the *imago Dei* is expected to serve as an intellectual tool to tease out the core meaning of being human for all humankind.

The four frameworks each elucidate different aspects of the *imago Dei* in distinct ways, and each of the four interpretations is a hermeneutical lens through which to explicate the implication of humanity as the *imago Dei*. The four lenses are not independent of each other and can team up to shape deeper analysis of the *imago Dei*. However, what remains to be explored is how they may converge to yield a fuller, richer account of the *imago Dei*. A holistic account of the *imago Dei* will be developed to integrating, rather than overriding, the four conventional hermeneutical frameworks. With this in mind, the principal argument advanced herein is that the *imago Dei* is the motivator within humanity for the narration of both God-human stories and stories of human ethical performances towards others and the signifier of the two categories of narratives that are inextricably related. This interpretative framework is premised on the theological claim that the *psychosomatic* human being acts as the *image* or *ectype* of the divine archetype, which foregrounds the role of the whole human person in the narration of both religious and ethical stories. This is related not only to Christians who are renewed in the *imago Christi* but also to all human persons, particularly advancing dialogue between Christian believers and atheists.

The section proceeds in three parts. First, I engage with the holistic accounts of the *imago Dei* articulated in relevant literature, with a focus on how the Reformed concepts of archetype and ectype give shape to the understanding of the *imago Dei* as the psychosomatic human being. Second, I will spell out the *imago Dei* as the signifier of religious and ethical narratives, which carries the significance primarily for Christian communities. Finally, I will unpack the *imago Dei* as the motivator in human psychosomatic wholeness for the narration of religious and ethical stories, which serves to bring out the ontological and ethical implications of this theological theme within the general contexts outside of Christian circles.

3.1 Moving towards a Holistic Account

A claim has been made earlier that the essence of the *imago Dei* lies in God himself rather than in humanity. The image of *God* requires conceptual analysis, which functions as a prerequisite for any meaningful understanding of the *image* of God. The former is the theological foundation indispensable for the interpretation of the latter. As Ian McFarland (2001, 220) compellingly remarks, 'if we want to know what the *imago* is, we cannot proceed by looking within ourselves, but only by looking without, toward the God whom we cannot see clearly unless it is first granted that we should see'. The architecture and implications of the *imago Dei* should be framed and formulated with reference to God, who has revealed himself through his work.

Having said this, the theocentric conceptualisation of the *imago Dei* does not imply that human existence and life must be bracketed out in any discourse on this theological theme. James Barr (1993, 170) aptly observes that while the *imago Dei* is mainly employed to speak of God and cannot be identified as something intrinsic to human existence, 'by its own nature as a statement of *likeness*, this particular speech about God necessarily says a great deal about humanity'. The speech about humanity is derived from the speech about God, and so the core meaning of *imago* is determined by God's work *for* and relationship *to* humanity.

It is worth dwelling on the prepositions 'for' and 'to' here. Richard Briggs (2010, 111–126) registers that the image of God should be understood in the theological spectrum of Israel and the church, which in turn points to God who summons them to be his people. The canonical narratives of God's people lay a foundation for the formulation of the *imago Dei*. For all that Briggs situates the clarification on the *imago Dei* within the wider context of God's relationship to his people, this hermeneutical methodology does not reckon with God's relationship to humanity more broadly in terms of creation. In this regard, Claus Westermann's analysis (1994, 142–161) proves more comprehensive, as it attends to the created reality as the theatre for the performance of events between God and humans. I shall return to Westermann's position in Subsection 3.2. At this point, my emphasis falls on the enquiry into how human creaturely reality – that is, psychosomatic wholeness – is essential to God's work for and relationship to humanity. By doing so, a holistic understanding of the human being as the *imago Dei* will come to the fore.

The theological theme of the *imago Dei* cannot operate on its own but is instead interwoven with other doctrinal *loci* and concepts. This Element will engage with the Reformed theology of archetype and ectype to clarify how the human being as the *imago Dei* – which connotes human psychosomatic wholeness – participates in divine–human events. Archetype (ἀρχέτυπος) denotes the ultimate exemplar or original pattern, and ectype (ἔκτυπος), by contrast, signifies a copy, replica, or reflection of the archetypal source. These two terms belong together as a paired nomenclature and stand in a relation of original and mirrored. I have treated the two Reformed concepts at greater length in my earlier work for articulating a holistic account of the *imago Dei* while engaging with AI and digital technology

(Xu 2023a, 187–196; 2023b, 642–659; 2024, 29–36). In what follows, I will revisit the main contours of my position and recapitulate the key points, tailored to the purpose of this Element.

'Archetype' and 'ectype' featured in the medieval theology and became two important concepts in post-Reformation theology (see Muller 2003, 225–228). They have since stood in an intrinsic relation to the doctrine of God and creation. Franciscus Junius (1545–1602) was the first Protestant theologian to employ this nomenclatural pair to define two categories of theology: archetypal theology (*theologia archetypa*) and ectypal theology (*theologia ectypa*). 'Archetypal theology,' Junius (2014, 107) argues, 'is the divine wisdom of divine matters. Indeed, we stand in awe before this and do not seek to trace it out.' Following this, he lays out a few features of archetypal theology (Junius 2014, 108–110). It refers to whatever exists in God himself and is beyond human knowing. This divine wisdom is categorically different from human wisdom and knowledge of God and his work. Archetypal theology is incommunicable, uncreated, essential, absolute and most perfect, and infinite insofar as it exists in eternal simultaneity with God and his being by virtue of divine simplicity.

With that being said, Junius does not mean that the knowledge of God cannot be communicated to humans. In his position, it is the image of archetypal theology that is communicated. God's willingness to communicate gives birth to ectypal theology, which is the image of the divine wisdom of divine matters (Junius 2014, 113). For Junius, the fundamental distinction between archetypal and ectypal theologies is determined by God's creative work. By God's creation, ectypal theology is, by its nature, finite, communicated and *created*, whereas archetypal theology is indefinite, absolute, and *uncreated* (Junius 2014, 117). From this vantage point, it comes to be seen that archetypal and ectypal theologies safeguard the ontological distinction yet connection between human beings as creatures and God as creator.

Junius's theology of archetype-ectype played a significant role in the formation of Protestant theology in the post-Reformation era, even more so in the formulation of theological prolegomena.[24] However, few theologians put this conceptual pair together with the *imago Dei*. Francis Turretin's theological anthropology is a typical example in this respect. By virtue of the correlation of the *imago Dei* and archetype-ectype, he refers the *imago Dei* to the human being as the ectype of the divine archetype (Turretin 1992–1997, 5.10.3). Of particular significance in Turretin's argument is that the *whole* human being is the ectype of God. Neither the soul nor the body alone can completely image the

---

[24] For further on this, see Gerhard 2009, 22–24; te Velde 2015, 33; Van Asselt 2011, 103–131.

divine archetype. This line of reasoning lends support to the claim that the uncreated archetype creates the ectype of human psychosomatic wholeness in the *imago Dei* such that humans can receive the communicated wisdom of divine matters.

The theological triad of psychosomatic wholeness, ectype, and the *imago Dei* is underexplored in Turretin's work. On this front, Dutch Neo-Calvinist Herman Bavinck (1854–1921) makes a sustained effort to probe the theological triad in depth. Underlying his theological anthropology is the ontological rationale that the human being does not have or bear but rather *is* the *imago Dei*, which is the essence of humanity (Bavinck 2004, 530, 554). This rationale threads through Bavinck's work with the archetype-ectype thinking. Bavinck presents a detailed treatment of the theological triad with reference to the ontological rationale:

> ṣelem means 'image,' both archetype (*Urbild*) and ectype (*Abbild*); děmût means 'likeness', both example (*Vorbild*) and copy (*Nachbild*). The concept of 'image' is more rigid, that of 'likeness' more fluid and more 'spiritual,' so to speak; in the former the idea of a prototype predominates, in the latter the notion of an ideal. The likeness is a further specification, an intensification and complement of the image. 'Likeness' in itself is weaker and broader than 'image;' an animal has some features that are similar and common with humans, but is still not the image of the human being. 'Image' expresses that God is the archetype and the human being is the ectype; 'likeness' adds that this image corresponds in all parts to the original. (2004, 532)

Understanding the *imago Dei* through the conceptual lens of archetype-ectype arrives at a significant corollary that both the whole human person and humankind are the *imago Dei*. As the divine archetype is conceptually linked to simplicity, the mirrored human ectype is not divisible but united as a whole in an ultimate sense. As such, the body and the soul cannot be separated altogether for a living human being (Gen. 2:7), and the division between the body and the soul is death, which is alien to the creation narratives of Genesis 1-2. This corollary contributes further depth to the thrust of the holistic account of the *imago Dei* in two dimensions.

First, the human being as the psychosomatic whole is the *imago Dei* and ectype of God. As Bavinck (2004, 533) argues, 'the whole human person is the image of the whole Deity'. The image of the divine archetype is demonstrated in the human soul, psychic faculties, moral life, the body and embodiment, the destiny to be with God (Bavinck 2004, 555–561). The five factors together suggest that the whole human person as the *imago Dei* finitely and analogically reveals 'all that is in God' (Bavinck 2004, 561).[25]

---

[25] Hence, Bavinck (2004, 561) asserts that '[a]mong creatures human nature is the supreme and most perfect revelation of God. And it is that [revelation] not just in terms of its pneumatic side, but equally in terms of its somatic side; it is that precisely as human, that is, as psychic, nature'.

Second, Bavinck's correlation of the *imago Dei* and the archetype-ectype thinking generates a collective interpretation of humanity. Humankind is created in the *imago Dei*, suggesting that each human person is equally the *imago creata* and the ectype of God. However, no single human person can fully exhibit the profound meaning of the *imago Dei*.

> Still, even this creation in God's image of man and woman in conjunction is not the end but *the beginning of God's journey with mankind*. . . . Upon the two of them God immediately pronounced the blessing of multiplication (Gen. 1:28). Not the single human person, nor the man and the woman together, but only the whole humanity is the fully developed image of God, his children, his race. (Bavinck 2004, 577; emphasis added)

Accordingly, a fuller sense of the *imago Dei* should be unpacked within the human community and through the events between God and the human race. The human ectype as the image of the divine archetype is progressively actualised in God's journey with humanity towards human destiny. I will go into the details of this collective interpretation in the next section.

The Reformed thinking of archetype-ectype helps lay out the twofold connotation of the holistic account of the *imago Dei*. That is, the term 'holistic' denotes both individual psychosomatic wholeness and the collective nature of humankind, with the integration of the former into the latter. The *imago Dei* is the whole human person living with human fellows within community (moral life) while journeying with God (religious life) towards human destiny. In this way, the conceptual pair of archetype and ectype rules out individualistic interpretations of the *imago Dei*. The holistic account furnishes a hermeneutical framework into which the four conventional interpretations coalesce. The human person's journey with God requires the soul, reason, and other psychic faculties (the substantive framework) to perform certain functions (the functional framework) with embodied bodies. The journey is saturated with divine–human and human–human relationships, which alike proceed from God's relationship to humans and consequently involve humanity's relationships with one another and with all things existing in relation with God (the relational framework). The end of the journey reveals an eschatological nature, which is constitutive of both individual human person and human community (the eschatological framework).

The four conventional frameworks are, therefore, fused into the holistic account as an effective interpretative tool for understanding the *imago Dei*.[26] Having said this, what warrants further enquiry is the precise meaning the

---

[26] Recent studies suggest that a more holistic understanding should be developed to incorporate conventional interpretations of the *imago Dei* (e.g., Vainio 2014, 121–134).

imago Dei conveys in the holistic term for psychosomatic human beings. In the next two subsections, I will elucidate the *imago Dei* as both the signifier and the motivator in human psychosomatic wholeness.

3.2 The *Imago Dei* as the Signifier in Human Psychosomatic Wholeness

The holistic interpretation of the *imago Dei* cleaves to the principle of the psychosomatic wholeness of humanity, which is in line with ancient Hebrew anthropology that views the soul and the body as a synthesis (Dietrich 2023, 245–262; Westermann 1994, 150). The significance of the *imago* is by no means confined to the soul or the body, as it is determined by God and his relationship to and work for the whole human person and the human race. To be sure, human psychosomatic wholeness should be explored in tandem with the enquiry into God's journey with humans. I will return to this subject in the next section. At this point, I will look into how the journey is linked up with humanity in both the individual and the collective understandings of the *imago Dei*.

Westermann's exegesis of Genesis 1:26–28 presents us with a point of departure for interpreting God's journey with humanity. Following Barth's relational interpretation, Westermann (1994, 150–151) contends that the *imago Dei* qualifies the human being to be God's counterpart. Yet notwithstanding this, he builds on Barth's position with additional depth and details.

> The creator created a creature that corresponds to him, to whom he can speak, and who listens to him. The strength of this explanation is only seen when the question is put in another form. It is not one of many possible answers to the question: 'What is the image and likeness of God or in what does it consist?,' but an answer to the question: '*What is the meaning of this further determination in the account of the creation of human beings?*' It consists in determining further the nature of *the act of creation which enables an event to take place between God and humans*; it is not a question of a quality in human beings. (Westermann 1994, 157; emphasis added)

Like David Kelsey, Westermann presses the point that creation has its own value. However, they differ in that Westermann brings into sharp focus the created reality as the primary context for the interpretation of the *imago Dei*, whereas, as analysed earlier, Kelsey's hermeneutical methodology is primarily Christocentric. All the more important is that Westermann's argument is resonant with Bavinck's construal of human creation in the *imago Dei* as the beginning of God's journey with humankind. Westermann (1994, 157–158) makes a nuanced clarification, namely, that the journey is concerning an event between God and humankind.

Westermann does not flesh out the term 'event.' What are the implications of the event for humans? Is the event singular, or has it evolved to be plural? How is the event associated with humanity in particular and with the created reality broadly? In what way can we understand the event from the perspective of the *imago Dei* in the New Testament? David Fergusson's recent holistic interpretation of the *imago Dei* develops a theological heuristic for adding details to the event between the human ectype and the divine archetype.[27]

Fergusson (2017, 236–249) renders the *imago Dei* within evolutionary history, in which humans are linked to other life-forms while retaining human uniqueness.[28] The significance of the *imago* does not lie in human ontological property, nature, or attribute. As such, Fergusson (2013, 440–445) is critical of the substantive, functional, and relational understanding of the *imago Dei* and seeks to construct a holistic interpretative framework into which the three conventional interpretations can be fit. As will be seen, his holistic methodology also serves as a congenial home for the eschatological framework. Following yet adapting Westermann's analysis, Fergusson defines the *imago Dei* as the signifier pertinent to all events taking place between God and humankind.

> Genesis 1 represents a new prologue that was placed at the front of a composite work and which offers a programmatic summary that anticipates later themes.... The deliberate juxtaposition of image and likeness seems to confirm this more developed use of these related concepts. This, however, suggests that the *imago Dei* might be better understood as a marker or signifier of a history that will unfold than a substantive notion that is central to Hebrew anthropology. What it signifies is that human beings have a central and distinctive place in the story that is about to be told. They are to become the object of divine address and encounter in a wide variety of ways, beginning in Genesis 2 but extending to the history of Abraham and his seed. The story that is about to be narrated is the story of human beings and God, although other actors are also present – it is not only the God-human relationship that is constituted by the creation of heaven and earth. While the *imago Dei* signifies here our identity as God's covenant partners, what this entails will require subsequent narration in the stories of Noah, Abraham et al. (Fergusson 2013, 446)

---

[27] I will recap my previous engagement with Fergusson's holistic interpretation for constructing a holistic account of the *imago Dei* (Xu 2024, 25–29). Yet, the main points will be reconfigured and expanded for the purpose of this study.

[28] According to Fergusson (2018, 189), the linking between humans and other life-forms provides a stronger testimony to God's kaleidoscopic creation. In light of Richard Bauckham's (2010, 64–102) study on creation and ecology, such linking reveals that the human being is a member of the community of creation, which serves as a valuable tool for integrating biblical material relevant to creation as a whole in response to ecological concerns.

Four observations can be made with reference to this passage, and they can assist drawing the foregoing corollaries into a more developed construct for the holistic account of the *imago Dei*.

First, the *imago Dei* as the signifier of the God-human story – that is, God's journey with humankind throughout history – requires the agency of the psychosomatic human person. If the whole human being is the ectype of the divine archetype, then both humanity's psychic and physical elements are constitutive of human agency to perform the history of God's relationship to humans.[29] Human agency in relation to the signifier sheds light on the substance (psychosomatic wholeness), function (narrating God-human stories), relationality (God-human history), and the eschatological destiny of humanity. Taking these together, the agency of the psychosomatic human person in encounter with God exhibits the religious nature of human life and existence. As will be illustrated, this religious nature is in Christians and atheists alike.

Second, the God-human story signified by the *imago Dei* concerns all humankind and the entirety of creation. With Genesis 1 as the prologue and Genesis 2 as the beginning of God-human stories, creation as a whole provides multifaceted elements to make up the strands and plots of the unfolding God-human story. As the *imago Dei* and the ectype of the divine archetype, humankind occupies a central place in the story by virtue of their covenant partnership. It is worth noting that this does not lead to an anthropomonic portrayal of the relationship between humankind and the rest of creation, making humankind determinative of the value and existence of the other creatures. The subsequent stories after Genesis 2 involve ethical relations between humans and creation, which features 'mercy, kindness, and justice' (Fergusson 2013, 450). This interpretation incorporates the functional framework and orients it towards an ethical vista for the community of humankind and other creatures. All the more important is that ethical relationships are characteristic of human communal life and demonstrate the collective nature of the *imago Dei*. That is to say, the holistic account cannot restrain the implications of the *imago Dei* to individualistic confines as if each human person could fathom the meaning of being the image. As noted earlier, the conceptual pair of the divine archetype and the human ectype entails the corollary that the *imago Dei* cannot be fully understood apart from the human community. The God-human story is unfolding through all humankind over the course of history, yielding not only religious life but also ethical performances towards humans themselves.[30] Ethical

---

[29] Fergusson (2018, 228–229) maintains elsewhere that human agency should be understood in a holistic way.

[30] Michael Welker's Edinburgh Gifford Lectures *In God's Image* (2021) substantiate that ethical performances are essential for humanity being shaped in the *imago Dei*.

relationships shaped by the narration of the God-human story serve as the context for the actualisation of human relationality. At the same time, it comes to the fore that the inextricable bond between the religious and ethical stories is rooted in the being of humans.

Third, that the *imago Dei* signifies religious and ethical stories concerning the entirety of creation opens up a broader context for elaborating on the meaning of the *imago Dei* in the New Testament. It is theologically ill-grounded to subordinate Genesis 1-2 to the New Testament as if the worth of God's creation *per se* has been overturned and must be recreated through redemption. Fergusson's reconfiguration of the *imago Dei* as the signifier dismisses such an exegetical principle. 'Within the theology of creation,' Fergusson (2013, 449) argues, 'our being made according to the divine image simply points to those forms and conditions that characterize human life in community. These become the locus of subsequent divine address and interaction in Scripture, the setting for a drama that enfolds, including the form that the incarnation takes.' As such, the *imago Dei* as the signifier unveils the independent value of creation and, more importantly, lays a solid foundation for the exposition of the doctrine of the incarnation – that is, the hypostatic union of divinity and humanity that is the *imago Dei*. From this it follows that the new humanity in Jesus Christ testifies to the continuity of the God-human story, inaugurated in Genesis 2 and unfolding throughout history.

Fourth, the *imago Dei* as the signifier denotes the covenant partnership of humanity and reveals the covenantal essence of the God-human story. Fergusson expands Westermann's notion of the event between God and humans in terms of covenant. The covenantal portrayal of the *imago Dei* strikes a chord with the notion of personhood as covenantal humanness in the Old Testament (Brueggemann 2005, 450–491). The covenant signified by the *imago Dei* strings together all stories of God and humans, dismissing the explicit distinction between the old and the new covenant and any attempt to downplay the value of the old one. The covenantal event between God and humans is, by its nature, singular, namely, the covenant of grace.[31] In other words, the story of God and humans commencing in Genesis 2 and subsequent stories throughout history belong into the covenant of grace. As Bavinck rightly notes, God's covenant with Adam in the form of the command shares with all subsequent

---

[31] Francis Turretin (1992–1997, 2.12.5) elucidates the unity of the covenant of grace and grounds it in the unity of the Trinitarian work. Clearly, the term 'the covenant of grace' is taken in a broader sense to refer to all God's covenantal relationships *to* his people. Hence, I would be reluctant to attribute the term 'the covenant of grace' solely to the covenant of salvation depicted in the New Testament as though God's work before the incarnation does not proceed out of his grace for creation. Rather, God's relationship to humankind and creation at large is rooted in his grace from the beginning to the end.

covenants between God and his people the same *telos* to shape human moral and religious life and lead them into eternal life (Bavinck 2004, 564–571). From this vantage point, it can be argued that creation has already pointed to the eschatological implication of the *imago Dei*. God's covenant with Adam is a beginning of God's journey with humankind, and the beginning is seminal and formative to the destiny of humanity.

> For when Adam falls Christ stands ready to take his place. The covenant of grace can replace the covenant of works because both are based on the same ordinances.... The traces of God (*vestigia Dei*) in creation and the image of God in humanity may be mangled and mutilated by the sin of the first Adam; but by the last Adam and his re-creating grace they are all the more resplendently restored to their destiny. The state of integrity – either through the fall or apart from the fall – is a preparation for the state of glory in which God will impart his glory to all his creatures and be 'all in all'. [1 Cor. 15:28] (Bavinck 2004, 588)[32]

Accordingly, humanity's identity as God's covenant partner showcases the unity of God's work *ad extra*. As the ectype of the divine archetype, the human being images God in both creation and salvation, which testifies to the covenant of grace between God and humans narrated from Genesis 2 onwards, particularly to the *imago Christi*, the true *imago Dei*.

The *imago Dei* as the signifier of the covenant of grace between God and humans adds much nuanced detail to the relationship between the *imago Dei* and human psychosomatic wholeness articulated in light of the archetype-ectype thinking. The covenant of grace demonstrates that the holistic account of the *imago Dei* is more aligned with the unity of God's work *ad extra* than the four conventional frameworks as examined in Section 2. Furthermore, the signifier of the covenantal events between God and humans running through history enables the *imago Dei* to carry religious and moral significance beyond Christian communities into quotidian life. 'Our image of God in everyday existence,' Fergusson (2013, 450) aptly remarks, 'is not confined to some religious province of life but is expressed in a multitude of human practices, institutions, and forms of life.' I will revisit this subject in Section 4.

Reading the *imago Dei* as the signifier of God-human stories in tandem with the human psychosomatic wholeness provides an analytical and integrative adhesive for coalescing the conventional four frameworks. The human being as created in the *imago Dei* is endowed with unique capacities

---

[32] The term 'the covenant of grace' is used by Bavinck here in a narrower sense, referring particularly to the new covenant described in the New Testament. However, he also uses the same term in a broader sense and argues that there is the same covenant of grace in the Old Testament and the New (Bavinck 2006, 223–228).

to narrate God-human stories and thereby the stories of ethical performances towards others (the substantive framework), revealing the uniqueness of humanity as the ectype of the divine archetype. Given that the God-human story extends to the entirety of creation, the unity of the religious and ethical implications of the *imago Dei* signifies that psychosomatic human persons should ethically perform their priestly agency to bring God's blessing to all creation (the functional framework), which is the narration of both religious and ethical stories inaugurated in Genesis 2. In this way, the holistic account reshapes the notion of human dominion over nature in that this function or regency rests with the human performance of both religious and ethical stories. The holistic account of the *imago Dei* as the signifier is, by its nature, characterised by relationality, extending the conventional functional framework to encompass not only God-human and human–human relationships but also the relationship between humans and all creation. Psychosomatic human persons are created to perform the multi-layered aspects of relationality in their religious and quotidian life so as to mirror the divine archetype (the relational framework). Given the *imago Dei* as the signifier, what is signified by the image has yet to be fulfilled, which means that psychosomatic humanity is created to participate in the unfolding of the covenant of grace until the eschaton (the eschatological framework). Coupled with the archetype-ectype thinking, the *imago Dei* as the covenantal signifier reveals the uniqueness of psychosomatic humanity participating in the narration of both God-human stories and stories of ethical performances towards others.

3.3 The *Imago Dei* as the Motivator in Human Psychosomatic Wholeness

The holistic account of the *imago Dei*, developed thus far, situates psychosomatic humanity within the narration of God-human covenants. This hermeneutical strategy is predicated on the independent value of creation and affirms that the value should be safeguarded by virtue of the unity of God's work while explicating the renewal of the post-fall *imago Dei* and the new humanity in Jesus Christ. From this it follows that each human person as the *imago Dei* is the narrator of the covenant between God and humanity. Her body and soul together participate in the narration of the story of God's journey with humankind. This Elysian portrayal of the *imago Dei* prompts the question of whether an atheist is still the *imago Dei*, because it is ludicrous to contend that atheists narrate God-human stories.

It proves challenging to define 'atheism', as its meaning has varied across historical contexts and communities.[33] Yet the variants of atheism are, by and large, classified into two categories: positive atheism (disbelief in or active rejection of God's existence) and negative atheism (the absence of belief in God's existence).[34] Either positive or negative atheism necessitates human psychic activities (e.g., volitional decision-making in not believing or refraining from belief in God or gods) and displays a form of moral praxis without relying on a theistic concept of objective moral standards (see Brink 2007, 149–165). In this light, the psychic and physical elements of humanity seem to co-operate to decline the narration of God-human stories insofar as God's relationship to humanity appears to have been ruptured. Indeed, it should be conceded that the holistic interpretation of the *imago Dei* as the signifier would, on the whole, carry little hermeneutical weight in an atheistic context.

It should be clarified at this point that atheism as such does not preclude the exploration of the *imago Dei*. At the first glance, the holistic account of the *imago Dei* – which stresses the participation of the psychosomatic human person in the narration of God-human stories – conceptually clashes with atheism, whether positive or negative. However, engaging with atheism will constructively articulate how atheism may lend support to the holistic account of the *imago Dei*. The theological theme of the *imago Dei* does not stand in a zero-sum relation to atheism. We need to circle back to the aforementioned theological motif underpinning our understanding of the *imago Dei*: the meaning of *imago* is, at its core, determined by God's work for and relationship to humanity. That is to say, notwithstanding that the notion of the *imago Dei* as the signifier becomes less effective in atheistic contexts, the holistic account – which is intended to convey the significance of the *imago Dei* beyond Christian circles – can still be relevant to atheists provided that the doctrine of God is foregrounded in the unfolding story of God and humans. The *imago Dei* itself is involved with a conceptual dimension proceeding from God and extending beyond the signifier. In this respect, Katherine Sonderegger's Christian dogmatic work on the doctrine of God offers a valuable resource for the holistic account developed in this Element.

Sonderegger articulates the theology of divine hiddenness based on the doctrine of divine unicity, which is the all-controlling principle guiding the formation and formulation of the doctrine of the Triune God (Sonderegger 2015, xv).

---

[33] For a helpful historical survey of the term 'atheism', see Fergusson 2009, 15–33.
[34] For further on the categories of atheism, see Walters 2010, 9–31.

> The Oneness presented to us on Horeb is marked out by its contrast with the visible, formed, and figured: the negative correlate to Oneness is the idol, the similitude fashioned out of the likeness of creatures. This means that God's Unicity is a predicate of annihilating concreteness, of a 'positivity' more direct and affirmative than any creaturely definition – and in just this way, a predicate of deepest mystery and negation. (Sonderegger 2015, 24)

Divine unicity undergirds God's radical distinction from creature and thus divine uniqueness, which in turn places God as the hidden in opposition to all creatures. However, while remaining a divine mystery, divine unicity does not lead to an agnostic notion of God. Sonderegger contests that 'God is Real *in* our encounter with Him, and in *just this way* is exceeding Mystery, superabundant Light' (Sonderegger 2015, 42; emphasis added). To be sure, she underwrites the dialectic of divine revealedness and hiddenness. It is in the divine–human encounter that God's hiddenness is revealed to human beings.

Having fleshed out the unicity of the revealed, yet hidden, God, Sonderegger leverages the theological theme of divine hiddenness to demonstrate that atheism does not invalidate the belief in God. She maintains that 'atheism testifies to the truth of the One God, his invisible Deity and Power, because God will not be left without His witnesses – even here, even in indifference and defiance' (Sonderegger 2015, 53).[35] It is the modern university and its academic training that Sonderegger attends to while engaging with atheism. Modern intellectual pursuit and academic research do not regard the idea of God as a necessary portion of their own, nor is its methodology partly dedicated to tackling the question of 'the Reality of God' (Sonderegger 2015, 56). In response to this methodological atheism, Sonderegger draws on the natural theology developed in William Paley's and Augustine's works. Although Paley's watch leads to a completely naturalised view of the world and fails to capture the full sense of God the creator, the natural mechanism he brings forth, nevertheless, enables us to focus on human distinctiveness and to explore things beyond mechanised humanity and world (Sonderegger 2015, 57–62). Unlike Paley's attention to the visible world, Augustine turns our attention to the human mind. Integral to Augustine's position is the claim that the mental introspection and thinking would lead humans beyond what can be seen and

---

[35] Clearly, Sonderegger takes a *ratio contraria* to J. L. Schellenberg's philosophical argument from divine hiddenness for atheism (Schellenberg 1993, 2015). According to Schellenberg, a perfectly loving God must always be relating to all finite persons who are not nonresistant nonbelievers. However, there are finite persons who are nonresistant nonbelievers, and so no perfectly loving God exists, which in turn indicates the non-existence of God. For a theological and critical engagement with Schellenberg's argument, see Rea 2018, particularly 13–28. There is no mention of Schellenberg in Sonderegger's work. However, Sonderegger's theological articulation of divine hiddenness is a compelling dogmatic response to Schellenberg's concept of nonresistant nonbelief in virtue of the dialectic of God's revealedness and hiddenness.

sensed and orient them to God (Sonderegger 2015, 63–64). As such, God is invisibly present in both the material and the spiritual (or intellectual) realm in the way that his presence 'is compatible with the creature's entire and exhaustive worldliness' (Sonderegger 2015, 65).

Sonderegger's work casts a spotlight on two ways to contemplate creaturely reality. Atheism looks at creation within creaturely confines, making creaturely reality independent of any belief in the transcendent. By contrast, (natural) theology examines creaturely reality and then looks to the realm beyond human sense perception. The concurrence of the two perspectives suggests that an atheistic approach to creaturely reality cannot falsify the theological one. Of greater importance is the potential interaction between the two perspectives in understanding creaturely reality. Atheism is resonant with the theological contemplation of creaturely reality precisely because the former often yields a form of spirituality, which pursues non-theistic search for the sacred and the infinite in order to transcend human finitude. For this reason, Walters (2010, 157–177) asserts that theists and religious believers can learn from atheism about how to take a closer look at the natural world while keeping their faith in the transcendent being. Sonderegger's work points us to another benefit that atheism can supply to Christian theology of creaturely reality. That is, atheism testifies to the hidden-yet-revealed God, who is the hidden one revealed through his Word. This corollary can open up a way to advance the holistic account of the *imago Dei* within an atheistic context.

The construal of *imago* is determined by the hidden and revealed God. As the ectype of the divine archetype, the psychosomatic human person is the image of God who is hidden yet revealed to his creatures. With this theological lens, the holistic account can be reformulated and expanded into two interrelated lines of reasoning. In terms of revealed God, the *imago Dei* is the signifier in human psychosomatic wholeness on the ground that the human person is the active narrator of God-human covenantal stories. Seen from the perspective of divine hiddenness, the human person images the hidden God who is invisibly present, and in this sense an atheist is the *imago Dei*. What is the *imago Dei* when divine hiddenness is imaged? Given the determination of God's relationship to and work for humans in this regard, the *imago Dei* qua imaging the hidden God should convey how an atheist unwittingly participates in the narration of stories between humans and the *invisibly present* God. This boils down to the question of how an atheist inadvertently testifies to the hiddenness of the revealed God, and the testimony itself points to the revelation of the hidden God. In this connection, cognitive science comes to play a constructive role.

Cognitive science of religion (CSR) has brought important resources to the explanation of religion as natural (or the naturalness of religion).[36] Following the findings of cognitive science, CSR declines the idea of the human mind as the *tabula rasa* but rather stresses humanity's intrinsic cognitive capacities and mechanisms for religion. Humans possess natural intuitions for religious beliefs. In CSR, beliefs do not denote a set of propositions or doctrinal formulas, which are explicit and derived from reflection on religious faith within particular cultural and communal contexts. These explicit beliefs accounts for the variety of beliefs across time and religious communities. For CSR, a belief is intuitive, implicit and nonreflective, referring to 'an instance of mentally representing something as being the case in the generation of further thought and action' (Barrett 2011, 40; also see Barrett and Lanman 2008, 109–124; Boyer 2022, 56–59). Rather than dealing with religion as a whole or the essentialist understanding of religion, CSR attends to the role that human cognitive systems have to play in recurrent and cross-cultural religious beliefs and practices.

CSR operates on a basic tenet that the naturalness of human cognitive systems exhibits the commonness of religion across cultures and communities, demonstrating that religion is an ingredient in human evolution.[37] It is worth pausing here to address the query about the extent to which CSR lends credence to the validity of religion, because cognitive science can also be employed to undergird atheism (e.g., Bainbridge 2010, 79–93). Religious beliefs may be either the product of cognitive biases or the by-product emerging as a beneficial adaptation during human evolution. The two positions are used to explain away religion and invalidate theistic belief (see van Eyghen 2016, 966–982). Be that as it may, it has been argued that theism or theistic belief is more cogent and adequate than atheism in explaining the human supernatural disposition, life's purpose, and other aspects of humanity (e.g., Braddock 2018, 171–198; Willard and Norenzayan 2013, 379–391). Following this line of thought, the theology of the *imago Dei* will add a greater sense to the naturalness of religion. More specifically, it can be argued that the naturalness of both human cognitive systems and religion refers to somethings stemming from the *imago Dei*. I will flesh out this observation anon. At this point, the focus is placed on the following question: How would CSR respond to atheism? If religion as natural lends credence to the universality of religion, then the identity of 'genuine

---

[36] De Cruz (2016, 481–493; see also De Cruz and De Smedt 2015, 19–39) helpfully examines how CSR's methodological naturalism demonstrates the naturalness of religion in response to metaphysical, phenomenological, and developmental naturalness.

[37] This rests with how religion is defined in CSR; see Barrett and Trigg 2014, 1–15; McCauley 2011, 145–221; White 2018, 35–49. On the critique of CSR's definition of religion, see, e.g., Reich 2009, 280–299.

atheist' collapses. On the other hand, atheism seems to imply that religion is not so natural as CSR suggests. This in turn undermines the holistic account of the *imago Dei* in the collective sense on the ground that some human persons either actively reject or simply lack beliefs in God or gods. To put it differently, these people are indifferent to or categorically reject the narration of God-human stories.

Much ink has been spilled on whether or not CSR is relevant to or compatible with atheism. Jonathan Lanman (2013, 489) registers that 'the cognitive sciences ... provide new, empirically grounded visions of the mind that can be used in accounts of atheism'. Here the distinction between explicit/reflective and implicit/nonreflective beliefs comes into play, which can be illustrated by a recent behaviour study undertaken by Victoria Alogna, Jesse Bering, and their colleagues (2019, 58–68). This study centres on humans' physiological responses to supernatural things (e.g., soul, the afterlife) when human participants receive religious stimuli (e.g., being informed of the existence of a ghost in the room). The result shows that human participants' physiological fear responses are not indexed to their self-reported beliefs (i.e., explicit beliefs). Those who receive religious stimuli demonstrate stronger physiological fear responses, regardless of their self-reported beliefs in the supernatural. While participants' explicit beliefs vary (atheistic or theistic), their physiological fear responses point to their implicit and nonreflective beliefs in the afterlife and the supernatural, which are unveiled with the change of circumstances.[38]

That being so, CSR is compatible with atheism in that atheism is associated with explicit and reflective beliefs, which may shift alongside changing external circumstances. The linking between atheism and external circumstances has also been proved by studies on relationship between religious belief and existential security. For example, Lanman (2013, 493) points out that the improvement of existential security and socio-economic quality leads to the decline of theism. Echoing Barrett's (2004, 108–112) position, atheists turn away from their natural cognitive mechanisms and nonreflective beliefs with the formation of reflective beliefs in response to certain circumstances. As such, the naturalness of religion primarily ties in with implicit and nonreflective beliefs, and atheism is not so natural as it may appear on the surface.[39]

How does the correlation of atheism and explicit beliefs allow for the theological theme of the *imago Dei*? It should be conceded that cognitive science does not generate data that straightforwardly showcase the *imago Dei*. Having said this, recent research on the quintessence of the human person, along

---

[38] For further on explicit and implicit beliefs, see Bering 2002, 263–308.

[39] Atheism can also be viewed as natural in the sense of practised naturalness, which requires special cultural scaffolding and practice (Barrett 2010, 169–172).

with the concept of implicit beliefs, lends substantial support to the holistic account of the *imago Dei* within an atheist context. According to Rebekah Richert and Kirsten Lesage (2022, 90–109), a large body of research has indicated that the formation of human identity not simply involves the body and the mind but is also associated with something essential to humans, which endures into the afterlife. The essential thing is called the quintessence of the human person and underlies our cognition and conceptualisation of other humans as well as religious beliefs. In this light, the quintessence signals humanity's natural tendencies towards religion and serves as a sine qua non for implicit beliefs. Given the distinction between explicit/reflective and implicit/nonreflective beliefs, this corollary remains valid for atheists.

The quintessence of humanity is often understood as the soul or spirit. However, the definition of 'quintessence' and the account of its function are open-textured and retain the conceptual elasticity. Viewed from Christian theological perspectives, the quintessence can be essentialised into or even as the *imago Dei*. By virtue of the *imago Dei* as the essence of humanity, the human being's natural tendencies towards religion, underpinned by cognitive capacities and mechanisms, are operative in both atheists and theists. In the scenario of atheism, implicit beliefs are overridden and, so to speak, God is hidden from human explicit beliefs. An atheist is the image of the *hidden-yet-revealed* God and testifies to divine hiddenness. In the scenario of theism, implicit beliefs 'inform reflective beliefs ... by lending credibility to reflective propositions' (Barrett 2011, 50). A theist is the image of the *hidden-and-revealed* God. With the *imago Dei* as their quintessence, both atheists and theists narrate the story of God and humans, though their narration is performed in their own ways.[40]

The detailed treatment of the *imago Dei* and atheism, informed by CSR, has corroborated that the notion of the *imago* as the signifier does not capture the full depth of the meaning of the *imago Dei*. Since human natural tendencies towards religion are rooted in humanity's quintessence, the *imago Dei* can be conceptualised as the motivator for the narration of God-human stories. It drives humans to narrate their religious belief in varying circumstances.

> Our natural tendencies towards religious belief and practice develop into a sense of trust and dependence on what lies beyond us. In this outward movement, we encounter a correlative movement of God towards us. This interaction shapes and directs our forms of life. We do not begin with a clear and distinct idea of God and probably cannot attain one, *but our naturally evolved religious tendencies may provide the setting for divine disclosure*. In

---

[40] Identifying the *imago Dei* with the quintessence of the human person resonates with studies on CSR and general revelation (e.g., Barrett 2011, 161–162; Sutanto 2025).

this way our nature can be said to find its fulfilment through grace. (Fergusson 2024, 1165; emphasis added)

Whilst the *Deus pro nobis* is always moving towards humans with divine grace, his image is motivated to respond to the divine movement with naturally evolved capacities rooted in the quintessence of humanity, though human responses vary due to their differing or even discrepant explicit beliefs.

How shall we construe the discrepancy between atheistic and theistic explicit beliefs in light of the *imago Dei* as the motivator? This question cannot be addressed without reference to the doctrine of sin and the fall. The doctrine of original sin can help play out the meaning of the motivator. It teaches that the sin of the earliest humans elicited noetic effects, resulting in the decline of the human knowledge of God and, consequently, of good and evil.[41] As per CSR, a compelling argument can be advanced that the noetic effects corrupted human cognitive mechanisms and subsequently eroded human natural tendencies towards religious belief. This accounts for the discrepancies between implicit and explicit beliefs, and between atheistic and theistic explicit beliefs. As such, I propose that there are three states of the *imago Dei* as the motivator. Before the fall, the *imago Dei* was *activated* as the motivator within humanity for and as the signifier of religious and ethical stories – corresponding to the creation narratives of Genesis 1-2, from which these stories have since been unfolding. After the fall, the *imago Dei* as the motivator was *deactivated* and entered a quiescent state, manifesting only in occasional bursts and thereby resulting in human inertia in narrating the stories of human ectypes and the divine archetype, which, nevertheless, testifies to divine hiddenness. By virtue of the renewed humanity in Christ, the *imago Dei* is the *re-activated* motivator for and the renewed signifier of the narration of religious and ethical stories. The re-activated motivator will be fully rejuvenated within the eschatological new humanity, which has been fulfilled in Jesus Christ. Due to the limited space of this Element, a further fine-grained investigation is required to enquire into the subtleties of each of the three states. For the time being, it can be argued that the

---

[41] Evolutionary theory has been utilised to challenge the theological viewpoint of the noetic effects of original sin (e.g., De Cruz and De Smedt 2013, 49–66). For a compelling response to these challenges, see Peels, van Eyghen, and van den Brink 2018, 199–214. This Element does not aim to examine in depth the relation between the *imago Dei* and the doctrine of the fall with reference to human evolution, which is beyond the present scope and warrants extensive treatment. While discussing the holistic account of the *imago Dei*, my purpose in bringing the fall into discussion is rather to spell out how the *imago Dei* as the motivator is construed in view of the noetic effects of the fall on humankind as a whole. On how the traditional (largely Augustinian) theology of the fall may be reconfigured in terms of human evolution, see, e.g., Bimson 2009, 106–122; Deane-Drummond 2017, 23–47; van den Brink 2020, 180–195. For enquiry into questions related to the *imago Dei*, the fall, and evil, see a number of articles in Rosenberg et al. 2018, 111–330.

three states together underwrite the claim that every human person as a psychosomatic whole, including atheists, is the *imago Dei*.

3.4 Summary

The holistic account of the *imago Dei* articulated in this section displays its integrative capability to synthesise and go beyond the four conventional frameworks on the one hand and, on the other hand, gives birth to a hermeneutical tool for incorporating atheists into the community of the human ectypes of the divine archetype. In other words, having merged the four frameworks into the holistic account, the concept of the *imago Dei* is made intelligible outside Christian communities, revealing that psychosomatic humanity mirrors the divine archetype in its being and action. The *imago Dei* as both the signifier and the motivator requires that both the psychic and the bodily aspects of humanity come into operation in the narration of religious and ethical stories. In this light, human uniqueness is inextricably associated with psychosomatic humanity as God's covenant partner and with derived ethical performances.

Despite depicting the core features of the holistic account of the *imago Dei*, this section leaves two matters in need of further exploration. For all that the holistic account stresses human psychosomatic wholeness in the narration of religious and ethical stories, it has yet to be investigated how the psychic and bodily aspects of humanity cooperate to narrate these stories such that the psychosomatic human person as the ectype acts as the covenantal partner of the divine archetype. Furthermore, the holistic account has demonstrated its value in carrying the implications of the *imago Dei* into a broader context beyond Christian communities. Yet, what remains underexplored is how these implications may be deployed within contexts beyond Christian circles.

4 The *Imago Dei* in Science-Engaged Theology

The *imago Dei* as both the signifier and the motivator puts a spotlight on psychosomatic humanity as the ectype of the divine archetype and accentuates the religious and moral implications of being the *imago*. The principal takeaway point is that all humankind participates in the narration of both God-human stories and the stories of ethical performances towards others. The ways in which these stories are unfolding and being narrated by psychosomatic humans call for further enquiry.

Given that the sciences investigate human beings and the natural, social, and cultural worlds they inhabit, scientific findings can be conducive to addressing the two matters left at the end of the preceding section. I will employ the rationale of science-engaged theology – subsumed within theology of science (Harris 2024, 13–39) – to illustrate how religious and ethical stories are respectively narrated. Theology of science emphasises 'the intricacies of the natural sciences as perceived from within a theological context' (Harris 2024, 25). For the sciences are considered a part of experience that acts as a source for theology (Perry and Leidenhag 2021, 248). From this reasoning, it follows that the sciences are a source for the theology of the *imago Dei*.

This section seeks to enquire into how the psychosomatic human person participates in the narration of religious and ethical stories within and beyond Christian communities, respectively, from the perspectives of neuroscience and AI. To be clear, neuroscience and AI cannot fathom the significance of the *imago Dei* for our religious and moral life. Rather, the two branches of technoscience offer case studies on how religious and ethical stories – signified and motivated by the *imago Dei* – are playing out in certain spheres of human life. Exploring neuroscience and religion is intended to unveil how the psychosomatic human person – particularly the human body – narrates the covenantal stories of God and humans. An enquiry into AI with a focus on AI ethics and empathy is aimed at representing a way in which humans narrate the stories of their ethical performances towards others. The convergence of the two lines of argumentation showcases that the *imago Dei* signifies religious and ethical stories and motivates humans to narrate these stories within and beyond the circle of Christianity.

It will be argued that both the religious and ethical significance of the *imago Dei* are embedded within humanity, which suggests that the psychosomatic human person has a disposition towards both religion or spirituality and ethical performances towards others. In what follows, I will first examine neurotheology, particularly looking at the challenge caused by atheism to the theological theme of the *imago Dei*. Next, I will enquire into ethical issues related to AI with a focus on empathy. These two subsections together will demonstrate how the theological theme of the *imago Dei* carries enduring relevance to all humans and to the multifaceted dimensions of human life.

4.1 The Brain Sensing the Divine Archetype

A great deal of work has been produced to bring neuroscience and religion into dialogue. A substantial portion of these studies is concerned with how neuroscience (e.g., neuroimaging and electrophysiological recordings) may be conducive to understanding religious beliefs, experiences, and spirituality. It is worth pausing here to clarify that interdisciplinary interaction between neuroscience and religion does not simply result in a reductive physical account of humanity, which reduces the spiritual to physical particulars in the brain as though there is a specific area in the brain like V.S. Ramachandran and Sandra Blakeslee's 'God module' (Ramachandran and Blakeslee 1998, 174–198), making humans wired to religion. This reductive physical account tends towards a substantive interpretation of the *imago Dei* and runs the risk of downplaying the value of other dimensions of human existence, as sketched by the other three conventional interpretations of the *imago*. On the contrary, such interaction can help to elucidate how the brain, as a particular part of the human body, is involved in the formation of religious beliefs and spirituality of the psychosomatic human person.

With the advent of neurotheology, scholars take pains to develop intersections between religion and spirituality on the one hand and neuroscience on the other hand, in order to discover the connection between human religious actions and the working of the brain. James Ashbrook (1984, 331–350) examines human responses to God's redemption and creation in relation to the distinct operations of the left hemisphere and the right hemisphere.[42] Whilst maintaining the unity of the function of the brain, he observes that the left hemisphere and the right hemisphere assume different roles in human response to God's action. The left takes the lead in human response to God's redemption and the proclamation of the word with vigilance and rationality, and the right in the human imagination of divine manifestation in creation with responsiveness and relationality. Ashbrook's emphasis falls not on the distinction between the two hemispheres but rather on human wholeness. 'By analogy,' he argues, 'God acts to make whole what is created whole in two ways. And human beings, made in the image of God (Gen. 1:26), participate in that power of whole-making' (Ashbrook 1984, 344). The left hemisphere and the right hemisphere are equally important for the whole human person as the *imago Dei* to respond to God's creative and redemptive work.

Neurotheology goes some way to opening the black box of spirituality and religious experience. The human subjective feeling of divine transcendence cannot be explained away in the psychic dimension and has an inextricable tie to human bodies. The human person's feeling of God's presence and religious response to God with words and actions are tied up with, for example, neurophysiological changes (e.g., Yaden and Newberg 2022, 72–92). This does not make neurotheology dominant in explaining religious experience and spirituality. Neurotheology can show how the human physical make-up involves in religious life, but it cannot account for other dimensions of religion, such as the

---

[42] It is worth noting that neurotheology does not aim to prove the existence of God. Rather, it seeks to disclose the meaning of God in human experience (Ashbrook 1996, 407–411; Newberg 2010, particularly 23–49).

naturalness of religion as brought to light by cognitive science of religion.[43] Furthermore, neurotheology requires theology to intervene more deeply in order to resist its tendency towards a materialist and reductive physical account of religion and human nature and draw out the theological meaning of neural activities as a particular part of the human person's bodily participation in religion.[44]

The holistic account of the *imago Dei* brings substantial theological depth in this regard. As the ectype of the divine archetype, the human being as a whole is motivated to narrate God-human stories. If the *imago Dei* is the signifier of these stories that have been unfolding since Genesis 2, then the brain, with its neural activity, should be construed as a part of that signifying matrix. As such, the human narration of God-human stories cannot be reduced merely to what happens in the conscious mind but rather requires the physical dimension of humanity to be operative in God's journey with humans. From this vantage point, two observations can be made concerning the holistic account of *imago*, as determined by God's work for and relationship to humanity.

First, neuroscience directs us to understand religious experience and spirituality in a wider community. Neurotheology associates neural activity with religious life, which is both individual and communal. It has been widely demonstrated that neuroimaging and other neuroscience techniques are used to display the connection between neural activity and individual religious life, such as meditation, prayer, and mystical experience. For example, functional magnetic resonance imagining has been utilised to detect that different cerebral areas and structures are associated with the distinct forms of meditation (Beauregard 2024, 632–653). As noted earlier, this neuroscientific finding reveals that human persons each are the psychosomatic whole while participating in the narration of God-human stories through unfolding of their personal existence and life, thereby rebutting reductive accounts that attribute spirituality simply and solely to the psychic dimension of humanity.

Apart from research undertaken at the level of the individual human person, neurotheological enquiry can also take place within the liturgical community. On this front, neuroscientific studies on the mirror neuron system bring much to the table. A great deal of scholarship consistently affirms that we have a mirroring brain, which has mirror neurons as a subset of visuomotor neurons and enables us to understand and imitate the behaviours of others (Rizzolatti and

---

[43] For a critical engagement with neurotheology from the perspective of CSR, see Visala 2015a, 1553–1568. Other challenges posed to neurotheology, see Dixon and Wilcox 2016, 91–107; Jastrzebski 2018, 515–524.

[44] For a critique of the materialist understanding of neural activities in relation to religious experience and spirituality, see Beauregard and O'Leary 2007.

Sinigaglia 2023, 1–37). The human mirror mechanism is of great important for our understanding of liturgy or communal worship. David Hogue's study on the liturgy from the neuroscientific perspective casts light on this subject. He argues that the neuroscientific portrayal of 'the brain as an organ of connection with others, of relationship' can help draw out the meaning of liturgy (Hogue 2006, 32). Underlying this bodily relationality is the human mirror mechanism, and it is inherent to the worshipper's participation in the liturgical community.

> Even more relevant to our practices of preaching and worship, ... hearing descriptions of actions stimulates not only the neurons responsible for speech (imitating the speech of the speaker), but even the motor neurons that would produce the actions being described. So when we are listening to a story or a sermon, our brains are mimicking not only the actions of the preacher or presider, but the actions of the characters in the stories being told. Either seeing or hearing an event prompts the brain to imagine its own body performing a particular action. (Hogue 2006, 36)

In Hogue's position, participating in communal worship does not simply originate in the psychic dimension, such as the human consciousness of God's presence within the liturgical community and the worshipper's sharing religious experience with others. Equally important is that the human body is created to enable the human being to be attuned to the experience of fellow worshippers. While placing the centre of gravity on the brain, the mirror mechanism serves to illustrate how the psychosomatic human being narrates the story of God and humans within the liturgical community. As per the theology of the *imago Dei*, communal worship signals the convergence of the *imago Dei* in the psychosomatic human person and that in collective humanity, testifying to the determination of God and *opus Dei pro nobis* in the holistic account of the meaning of being the *imago*.

The second neurotheological observation regarding the holistic account of the *imago Dei* is concerned with the work of God *in* the brain and the neuroscientific interpretation of the new humanity restored in conformation to the *imago Christi*. Neuroscientific research on the changes within the brain during spiritual practice lends credence to this perspective. Mario Beauregard and Vincent Paquette (2006, 186–190) use functional magnetic resonance imaging to discover the neural correlates associated with the contemplation of nuns who are members of the Carmelite Order. The results show that various brain areas are activated for different mystical experiences. For example, changes and activation in the superior parietal lobule (which is involved with our spatial orientation) observed during spiritual contemplation indicate an alteration of the body schema, taking place when the Carmelite nuns feel the experience of being absorbed into God. In like manner, Andrew Newberg and his colleagues

(2003, 625–630) utilise neuroimaging techniques to detect changes in cerebral blood flow when Franciscan nuns practise meditative prayer (verbal meditation). Coupled with meditative prayer is the increase of cerebral blood flow in the prefrontal cortex, inferior parietal lobes, and inferior frontal lobes.

The studies on neurological alterations related to spiritual practice turn down the dualistic divide between the brain and the mind, and between the body and the soul. What is felt during spiritual practice is bound up with the human physical make-up, demonstrating psychosomatic humanity in the narration of God-human stories through spiritual practice. The holistic account of the *imago Dei* can add theological detail to the meaning of these neurological alterations. Given that the *imago Dei* is determined by God's journey *with* and relationship *to* humankind, it can be argued that neurological alterations related to spirituality and religious experience originate from the nervous system, which is part of the psychosomatic human being created as the ectype of the divine archetype. To this extent, a bold claim can be made that the *imago Dei* signals the creation of psychosomatic humanity with biological mechanisms (parallel to cognitive capabilities and mechanisms as suggested by CSR) that motivate humans to narrate God-human stories. Therefore, relying upon extensive neurotheological research, Newberg and Waldman (2009, 49) argue that 'different parts of the brain produced different experiences that affected the way we perceive or think about God, the universe, our mind, and our lives'.

This corollary opens up a new path to give the biological texture to the new humanity restored after the *imago Christi*. The new life that believers receive through the restoration of the *imago Dei* is often construed as living in communion with God and thus behaving morally in the imitation of Christ. This new religious and moral life points to the eschatological new humanity promised in Jesus Christ. Theologians pay close heed to the religious, moral, and metaphysical implications of the new life. However, the preceding elaboration on the independent value of creation in reference to the *imago Dei* underwrites that elements of creation somehow continue into the *imago Dei* in Jesus Christ, which is restored towards the eschaton.[45]

If the holistic account of the *imago Dei* involves the biological mechanism of the nervous system for the human narration of God-human stories, then the eschatological new humanity in Jesus Christ must bear on the human person's biological capacities for the journey with God into eternity.[46] As David Kelsey

---

[45] John Polkinghorne (1994, 170) argues: 'Because modern physical understanding associates matter and spacetime intimately with each other, it is a natural to suppose that the "time" of the new creation bears some sequential relationship to the time of the old – it comes "after" or "beyond" that transformation of matter into "matter".'

[46] Given the limited space of this Element, further study is warranted on the biological body and resurrection. On relevant studies, see, e.g., Davis 2015, 293–302; Mugg and Turner 2017, 121–144; Zimmerman 1999, 194–212.

remarks, 'stories of God's creating have their own narrative logic which should not be ruled by the narrative logic of stories of God's drawing creation to eschatological consummation or by stories of God's reconciling alienated creation' (Kelsey 2009, 1:162). Both God's creation and redemption-resulted eschatological consummation are foundational to the human psychosomatic condition. Before proceeding further, it is worth noting here that research on neurological alterations related to religious life does not necessarily lead to a reductive physicalist or materialist understanding of religious experience as if religion is determined by the human biological condition. Malcom Jeeves (2017, 143) cautions that the believer's religious hermeneutical framework is essential for the religious meaning of her experience insofar as relevant neural activation within the brain is part of the whole brain cognitive system. Despite neural alterations implying a biological underpinning of religious experience and spirituality, it is naïve to claim that the brain causes religious experience precisely because a believer's religious faith cannot be construed outwith her particular religious tradition, community, and context, which endow religious belief and experience with specific meanings and value.

The neurological underpinning of spirituality and religious experience raises a question about atheism. How could atheists be indifferent to or actively decline belief in God if their nervous system as well as bodily make-ups are created with biological capacities to narrate God-human stories? Iain McGilchrist's work (2009) on the differences between the left hemisphere and the right hemisphere of the brain can help address this question. The right hemisphere takes on the primary role by virtue of its broad, vigilant, and open attention to wholeness, relationality, reciprocity, affections, and things as they are present before us. The left hemisphere is primarily concerned with the fragmentary representation of the visual world, the mechanical rearrangement of already-known things, and the manipulation of disembodied and isolated things that are present to the right hemisphere.[47] The two hemispheres are not completely divided but rather cooperate for the function of the brain. Despite this, following the survey of Western cultural history, McGilchrist (2009, 428–462) contends that the left hemisphere has been increasingly becoming dominant over centuries and continuously contributes to yielding a materialistic, mechanistic, and rationalistic worldview, resulting in the decline of Western religions.

McGilchrist (2009, xiv–xv) aims not to contest that the brain gives birth to human experience, culture, and the development of civilisation. Rather, he

---

[47] On the characteristics of the two hemispheres and their differences, particularly see McGilchrist 2009, 133–208.

seeks to bring to light the correlation between them. In his position, it is necessary to invoke the concept of God in order to 'ensure that we do not lose sight of the deepest of life's enigmas' (McGilchrist 2022, 1203). Furthermore, McGilchrist (2022, 1207) argues that 'a disposition towards God is largely dependent on the right hemisphere, the hemisphere that ... brings us closer to truth than the left'. Having foregrounded the primacy of the right hemisphere in religion, McGilchrist contends that

> as well as personal, the sense of the sacred is inevitably shared and communal; as well as being an inner realisation, it is realised externally in the visible, tangible, world; as well as being transcendent, it is immanent, having to do with the thisness of things in time and place, not just with abstract generalities. That is why there is not just my disposition or your disposition, but such a thing as religion. (2022, 1218–1219)

For all that McGilchrist's work largely pertains to Western contexts, his findings regarding the two hemispheres in relation to culture and religion fuel responses to the anticipated atheistic critique of the neurological underpinning of religious life, which, to put it in terms of the *imago Dei*, implies humanity's created biological capacities for the narration of God-human stories. Atheism has nothing to do with the biological nature of the brain. It would be misleading to argue that some humans are biologically destined to turn down beliefs in divine or transcendent beings. Atheism is associated with the predominance of the left hemisphere and the inferiorisation of the right hemisphere, and its development and varying manifestations should also be unpacked in tandem with particular cultures and contexts.

As the ectype of the divine archetype, the psychosomatic human being as the *imago Dei* is created to sense God and respond to God's work. For this reason, despite their indifference to or active rejection of belief in God or gods, atheists still pursue a form of spirituality to touch the transcendent (Antinoff 2009; Schnell and Keenan 2013, 101–118). Atheist spirituality is consistent with the religious implication of the holistic interpretation of the *imago Dei* in relation to human psychosomatic wholeness. Like the theological linking of the *imago Dei* and the quintessence of humanity as noted through CSR, neurotheology echoes the holistic account of the *imago Dei* by revealing that both the psychic and the somatic dimensions of humanity are involved in the narration of God-human stories. Viewed in this light, the *imago Dei* can be understood in a *substantive* sense on an ad hoc basis in that it implies the role of human biological make-up in their response to God. It also carries a functional connotation by virtue of the operation of the human body in narrating God-human stories. It is embedded with relationality insofar as humans are created with a natural disposition towards God, giving birth to spirituality and religious experience. Last but not least, it points to an eschatological renewal of humanity in both the biological and spiritual sense. This double renewal expands what is promised in Jesus Christ beyond the spiritual realm and, at the same time, endorses the independent value of creation vis-à-vis redemption and eschatological consummation.

Neurotheology has thus far been utilised to illustrate that the psychosomatic human being narrates God-human stories in terms of the holistic interpretation of the *imago Dei*. Scholars have extensively engaged with interaction between neuroscience and ethics (see, e.g., Churchland 2011; Gonzalez-Liencres, Shamay-Tsoory, and Brüne 2013, 1537–1548). In like manner, theologians also leverage neuroscience to advance constructive work in theological ethics (see, e.g., Messer 2017; Rhonheimer 2014, 1–17). Owing to the constraints of space, it warrants further enquiry into the capacity that theological neuroethics has to shed light on the claim that the *imago Dei* is both the signifier of the stories of human ethical performances towards others and the motivator for the narration of these ethical stories. For the purpose of this Element, I proceed to explore how ethical stories signified and motivated by the *imago Dei* may be imaged in our current AI-driven society.

4.2 Imaging Empathy in AI Systems

The full sense of the *imago Dei* cannot be captured without reference to the community of humankind on the ground that the human person's ethical performances towards one another presuppose communal life and flourishing. The ethical implication of the *imago Dei* is embodied in human quotidian life, on which the use of technology has had a significant bearing (see, e.g., Barbour 1993, Vallor 2016). In contemporary human society, the most influential and transformative technology is AI, which refers to 'a science and a set of computational technologies that are inspired by – but typically operate quite differently from – the ways people use their nervous systems and bodies to sense, learn, reason, and take action' (Stone et al. September 2016, 4). AI has saturated human society and life on all levels, ranging over transportation, education, national security, healthcare, and so forth. As such, it is unrealistic to explore how the ethical significance of the *imago Dei* correlates with the deployment of AI across all spheres of human life. In this subsection, I will explore the concept of empathy in relation to AI to illustrate how the stories of human ethical performances towards others can be narrated by AI-driven artefacts.[48] This

---

[48] It is worth noting that the holistic account of the *imago Dei* does not arrive at the corollary that only humans are empathic. Animals participate in the *imago Dei*, though the image in animals is different from that in humanity in degree. Deane-Drummond (2014, 307) helpfully observes: 'If, as I have suggested here, image bearing is as much about a particular performance in

enquiry can also help to showcase how the collective significance of the *imago Dei* can be mirrored in AI society insofar as empathy always takes place between humans and thereby within communal life.

The notion of empathic AI has been raised to articulate how AI-driven artefacts can be designed and used to promote empathic relationships between humans. Empathy reveals the human person's capacity to understand what other persons undergo and to show sympathy for them, which implies that the empathiser sees and interprets circumstances through the eyes of empathisees as if enduring the same adverse conditions. For this reason, empathy is a moral virtue, and its growth naturally leads to the consolidation and advancement of both morality and communal life.[49] Viewed from the theological perspective, empathy is a crucial aspect of the ethical implication of the *imago Dei*, enabling humans to narrate the stories of their empathic performance towards others. With this in mind, empathic AI means that the deployment of AI within human society serves for the cultivation of empathy as a virtue.

However, the recent rapid progress and widespread application of AI technology have produced the opposite effect. A tendency emerges that AI weakens the human capacity for empathic relationships owing to the replacement of human–human relationship with human–AI interactions. Shannon Vallor's recent work *The AI Mirror* furnishes a philosophical lens through which to grapple with this issue. The thrust of her argument is that AI is not a value-free technology but a mirror of humanity.

> Today's AI mirrors tell us what it is to be human, what we ourselves care about, what we find good, or beautiful, or worth our attention. *It is these machines that now tell us the story of our own past, and project our collective futures*. They do so without living even one day of that history, or knowing a single moment of the human condition. . . .. For we all stand on the brink of losing sight of the vast space that stretches between humanity and our machines. Unless we take bold steps to transform how we as human beings relate to the tools we have built, we may all end up . . . talking to ourselves in the AI mirror. (Vallor 2024, 3; emphasis added)

---

a theo-drama as ontology, then other animals in the likeness of God enter into that performance as participants in a shared relationship with human beings and are bound up with them. The difference between other animals and humans is that only the latter are capable of an awareness of their active role in their performance and in this sense are capable of using their minds to adapt to new possible futures. Inasmuch as other animals are not yet perfect, they are still capable of being transformed into a more perfected divine likeness, but this is through the work of grace in eschatological hope rather than in an expectation for present reality.' This aligns with the fact that many non-human animals exhibit empathy to some degree; see, e.g., Decety et al. 2016.

[49] For a cogent defence of the moral importance of empathy, see Maibom 2014.

Integral to Vallor's position is that AI as the mirror of humanity has distracted our attention away from our own understanding of humanity to the meaning of being human shaped by these intelligent machines. Worse still, this distraction results in the subordination of humanity to AI. This does not mean AI will replace humans and threaten human existence, as some science fiction and film allege. Rather, the distraction elicits 'an internal disorder' within humanity itself (Vallor 2024, 4). The consequence that follows is the loss of our understanding of the meaning of being human in AI–human interaction. As a result, there will be 'the gradual erosion of human moral and political confidence in ourselves and one another ... that humans are slower, weaker, less reliable, more biased, less rational, less capable, less valuable than our AI mirrors' (Vallor 2024, 200). Following Vallor's observation, a further step can be taken to argue that the erosion includes declining confidence in human empathy.

Coupled with the decline of confidence in the empathic relationship between humans is a shift in preference from the human–human relationship to the human–AI relationship, which is corroborated by prevalent relational artefacts, that is, computational products driven by AI systems to operate as companions by providing personalised company.[50] This shift is entangled with a form of behaviourism and materialism. Sherry Turkle strikes an insightful note on this matter.

> Today one does not linger over inner states. The new focus is on behavior. What matters is how the robots perform and how we perform for each other – the essence, after all, of life in virtual communities where we create an avatar and put it on a self-built stage. With the focus on behavior rather than inner states, a creature that behaves appropriately is an appropriate creature. (Turkle 2010, 8)

In Turkle's position, humanity, along with human–human relationships, is defined merely by visible behaviours and materialised in the virtual contexts that humans create. Despite that she makes the observation on digital companions in virtual environments, the underlying principles are equally applicable to AI companions. That is, empathic relationships between humans cannot be fully reproduced by silicon-based AI companionship precisely because human inner states and humanity on the whole cannot be simply reduced to the visible behaviours of artificial companionship.

The holistic account of the *imago Dei* has much to offer in dealing with such a kind of behaviourism and materialism. The psychosomatic human being as the *imago Dei* implies that the humanity as the ectype of the divine archetype forms the basis of the narration of the stories of human ethical performances towards

---

[50] For further on artificial companionship, see Wilks 2010; Xu 2024, 155–187.

others, not vice versa. Philip Hefner rightly remarks that 'being a person is constituted both by a cognitive process of perceiving and understanding oneself in one's world, and also by a moral process of responding in relationship to that world' (Hefner 2000, 84). In this light, the holistic account of the *imago Dei* theologically resonates with Vallor's concern about the erosion of the moral confidence in humanity. Specifically, the erosion reveals the dimming or de-activated state of the *imago Dei*, and foregrounding the *imago Dei* in the holistic sense can offer a remedy to the decline of confidence in empathic relationships.

The holistic sense of the *imago Dei* suggests that empathy is involved not only with one's consciousness and feeling of others or other psychic elements but also with the body. Empathic relationships between humans cannot be fathomed in the psychic dimension of humanity, and its irreplaceable nature is rooted – partly yet significantly – in the empathiser's body. As noted earlier, the narration of both religious and ethical stories demands the operation of both the psychic and somatic aspects of humanity insofar as the human being is indivisible and united as a whole by virtue of their being the ectype of the simple divine archetype. For this reason, as Carl Braaten and LaVonne Braaten (1976, 6) argue, 'a person does not have a body; he is his bodily being from crotch to crown. A person is also spirit, but always embodied spirit. He is also a piece of nature, a lump of the earth, from dust unto dust, as Genesis 3:19 puts it'. With the bodily embodiment we each distinguish from and relate to one another, belonging into the physical community of the *imago Dei*. As such, the body is a *condicio* sine qua non for empathy and performs empathic actions towards others, contributing towards moral growth and the flourishing of human life.

That being so, bodily action is indispensable for empathic relationships, and the growth of empathy requires the human being's persistent practice of bodily empathic actions. In terms of the holistic account of the *imago Dei*, the practice is a part of the narration of the stories of ethical performances towards others. In this connection, Andrew Graystone's observation is highly pertinent:

> Digitally mediated content can evoke very real responses, such as laughter, disgust or compassion. However, the collapse of context – the detachment from space and time – that is inherent in digital communication takes the subjects to an 'uncanny' area in which it is impossible to know whether what they are interacting with is 'real' or constructed....Technology opens a gap between the imaginative work of the mind and the physical expression of the body. (Graystone 2021, 157)

Two inferences can be made here. First, having substituted human–AI interaction for human–human relationship, the uncanny area makes empathisees unable to respond to emphatic relationship properly. The rupture of bodily interaction between empathisers and empathisees may lead the latter to mistake constructed and artificial empathic action for affective and cordial one. The collective implication of the *imago Dei* implies that the lack of the bodily interaction hardly engenders communal life, which is a prerequisite for empathy.

Second, worse still, the gap between imaginative empathy and bodily empathic action, derived from the substitute of human–AI relationship for human–human relationship, results in the empathiser's inertia in the practice of empathy. The gap, de facto, deprives the empathiser of her opportunity to practise empathy. Such empathic inertia illustrates a tendency towards moral deskilling. Shannon Vallor (2015, 107–124) reminds us that technology brings about a revolution in human practices, curtailing our opportunities to repeat the practices of moral skills under specific conditions and consequently becoming a hindrance to the growth of practical wisdom and moral virtue. In the scenario of AI–human interaction, empathic action is performed out of AI algorithms (mathematical operations) and is, by doing so, standardised and uniformised on a large scale. By contrast, empathy as a moral virtue requires practices to be repeated within varying social contexts and communal life.[51] From this vantage point, it can be seen that empathic action is not something that generates benefits to empathisees alone. On the contrary, empathic human–human interaction is, first and foremost, of benefit to empathisers. As per the holistic account of the *imago Dei*, performing empathic action towards others enables empathisers to experience the meaning of being human and to live out the meaning of the *imago* within communal life. In other words, the being of humans shines through human–human empathic interaction. It is through the repetition of empathic practices that the human person narrates her stories of ethical performances towards others.

Having unpacked the irreplaceability of human–human empathic relationship in light of the ethical significance of the *imago Dei*, the following question arises: In what way does the theological theme of the *imago Dei* contribute to the development and design of empathic AI? Addressing this question is of particular importance for the future of empathic AI, for there is the growing optimistic gesture to the deployment of AI to shape empathic relationships

---

[51] This follows Alasdair MacIntyre's definition of the practice of virtue: 'By a "practice" I am going to mean any coherent and complex form of socially established cooperative human activity through which goods internal to that form of activity are realized in the course of trying to achieve those standards of excellence which are appropriate to, and partially definitive of, that form of activity, with the result that human powers to achieve excellence, and human conceptions of the ends and goods involved, are systematically extended' (MacIntyre 2007, 187). The hindrance to the practice of empathy in the scenario of AI–human interaction causes ethical and mental issues (e.g., Kurian 2025, 132–139).

between humans. For example, Abootaleb Safdari (2025, 3123–3138) argues that humans can establish an empathic relationship with automata, engendering trust-based interaction between humans and AI. However, many scholars cogently argue that present AI systems are often endowed with more trust than is deserved (see, e.g., Reinhardt 2022, 735–744). The holistic account of the *imago Dei* can mitigate such over-trust while developing empathic AI in two respects.

First, the unique role of psychosomatic humanity rooted in the *imago Dei* exhibits that empathy *per se* cannot be reproduced or emulated but rather mimicked and simulated in AI systems.[52] AI is designed to mediate empathy between humans. In other words, AI–human interaction is reconfigured as an empathic relation between humans, that is, between AI developers as empathisers and end users as empathisees. For example, in the scenario of AI-driven pastoral care, it is the AI developer who takes on the role of principal empathiser. Ministers can be considered secondary empathisers insofar as they only participate in the predefined practical use of empathic AI. AI developers should understand and even foresee what end users may undergo and show sympathy for them, interpreting and addressing potential circumstances through the eyes of end users. By virtue of AI's voluminous data and extensive application across communities, the AI developer's empathic action can be amplified and expanded to reach empathisees far afield.[53] As such, AI extends the empathiser's psychosomatic empathic actions beyond her bodily limitations and serves as an artificial mediator that brings out the collective significance of humanity for our communal life. To this extent, it can be argued that AI augments the human person's capacity to narrate the stories of her ethical and empathic performance towards others.

Second, and of greater importance, the collective implication of the *imago Dei* offers an ontological apparatus through which to foreground the reason for the weaving of empathy into every phase of the development of AI systems. Empathic AI is resonant with the well-established concept of the AI ecosystem and its relevant dynamics. Bernd Stahl presents us with a concise definition of AI ecosystem: 'There are many different actors and stakeholders involved. These interact in complex ways with consequences that are difficult to predict. They are all mutually dependent, even though the disappearance of any one of them will not necessarily damage the overall system. They co-evolve and try to prosper' (Stahl 2020, 84). In this light, an ecosystem of empathic AI implies that

---

[52] John Puddefoot (1996, 66) draws a clear conceptual distinction between emulation and simulation; see also Xu (2024, 38–39).

[53] Therefore, it is human-like (not human-level) characteristics that are mediated through empathic action in different spheres of human life (e.g., Pelau, Dabija, and Ene 2021).

all actors and stakeholders should work together for the performance of empathic actions towards empathisees. Empathic AI is not only concerned with individual engineers but also with all people involved in the development of AI systems, be it data curators, AI architects, project managers, or other stakeholders. It is through these people that empathy is imaged into empathic AI.[54] While the AI ecosystem turns our attention to the necessity of the collective effort in cultivating empathy among communities, what remains unexplored is the question of what underlies and motivates AI-driven communal work for the growth of empathic relationship.

The holistic account of the *imago Dei* as the signifier of the stories of ethical performances towards others and the motivator for the narration of these stories sheds theological light on the ontological underpinning of the ecosystem of empathic AI. The *imago Dei* indicates each human person's innate capacity – endowed with at creation – to narrate the growth of empathy as a virtue. Furthermore, its collective significance brings to light the existential basis of an empathic AI ecosystem. That all actors and stakeholders of an AI ecosystem belong into the community of humankind serves as a precondition for the persistent consolidation of the mutual dependence and cooperation between these people. From this it follows that the ecosystem of empathic AI stands or falls with the flourishing of human communal life.

Concomitant with the existential basis is the teleological implication of the *imago Dei* as psychosomatic humanity. As noted earlier, the holistic account takes in and goes beyond the eschatological interpretation of the *imago Dei*. The history of humanity is not determined by humans themselves. That the *imago Dei* is the signifier of the history that has been unfolding since Genesis 2 suggests both that human history develops towards the divinely destined *telos* and that religious and that ethical stories play an equal role in this historical development. Therefore, the *imago Dei* points to an ethical vista that is beyond what human moral efforts can attain, and the human narration of ethical stories reveals the eschatologically oriented nature of humanity.

The eschatological character of human ethical life alerts us to over-optimism about the deployment of empathic AI to facilitate human ethical performances towards others and form technomoral futures. The rapid progress of AI technology may induce one to endorse a form of AI-solutionism, which prioritises AI as

---

[54] For example, Ramya Srinivasan and Beatriz González (2022, 5) argue: 'The incorporation of empathy in AI systems calls for creation and enforcement of new capabilities and requirements such as to consider subjective viewpoints of different stakeholders, to base decisions not only on proxy data, and to appeal across stakeholders. These requirements necessitate an understanding of all stakeholders' intentions and contextual information related to their affective states, intentions, and socialization patterns. Furthermore, empathetic AI systems should care for users' well-being, and demonstrate responsibility in decision making.'

the best, and even the only, solution to problems. Empathic AI is neither the best nor the only way to cultivate the virtue of empathy among human communities. Shannon Vallor (2016) cogently demonstrates that the growth of our virtue in the technological era is confronted with multiple challenges posed by the global technosocial power, which requires us to reconsider our virtuous life with technomoral wisdom.[55] In this respect, the eschatologically oriented nature of the *imago Dei* and its ethical significance remind us that human empathic action and moral practice at large cannot fully narrate the ethical stories of empathic relationships between humans. Therefore, it is naïve to hand over empathic actions like elderly care entirely to AI ecosystems.[56] For the future of human moral life is not constructed by humans out of the past moral life (i.e., data regarding moral behaviours) but is, theologically speaking, ultimately given by God through the new humanity in Jesus Christ, the true *imago Dei*.[57] The openness and receptiveness to an unpredictable and given future should guide each phase of the development of the ecosystem of empathic AI. As per the holistic account of the *imago Dei*, the openness and receptiveness vividly reflect the genuine humanity given at creation.

4.3 Summary

How can the religious and ethical implications of the *imago Dei* be extended beyond the context of the Christian faith? I have capitalised on neuroscience and AI to illustrate the religious and ethical nature of psychosomatic humanity – that is, the brain sensing the divine and empathy as indispensable for human existence in AI-driven society. The holistic account of the *imago Dei* adds detail to human psychosomatic wholeness from the perspective of the Christian faith, showing how God-human religious stories and human–human ethical stories depict the texture of human religious life and the ethical rationale for AI–human interaction.

The two case studies on the holistic meaning of the *imago Dei* extend the use of this theological theme beyond Christian contexts and bring to light the transcendent significance of a human person's religious and ethical life for all humankind. As the ectype of the divine archetype, the human brain is created

---

[55] For Vallor (2016, 154), technomoral wisdom is 'a general condition of well-cultivated and integrated moral expertise that expresses successfully – and in an intelligent, informed, and authentic way – each of the other virtues of character that we, individually and collectively, need in order to live well with emerging technologies'.

[56] On the critical analysis of AI-driven elderly care, see, e.g., Coin and Dubljević 2021, 553–569; Sharkey and Sharkey 2010, 245–255; Vozna and Costantini 2025, 30–40.

[57] I have argued elsewhere that it is the hope for the God-given future, rather than human planning for a future based on algorithmic work on data, that fuels the growth of human moral life (Xu 2025, 183–200).

with biological capacities to sense the divine and narrate the covenantal stories of humans and God, the capacities persisting even among atheists in their pursuit of spirituality. As the image of God, atheists are also motivated to narrate God-human stories in their own spiritual way, varying from Christian as well as other theistic narratives. By the same token, empathy is embedded within humans that belong into the community of the *imago Dei*. Human empathic action is irreplaceable and can be augmented by empathic AI to *both* extend our moral practice *and* sustain our openness and receptiveness to a given future, where humans share with their fellows and to which they are eschatologically oriented. This principle is of considerable import for the design of the ecosystem of empathic AI in mitigating over-trust in AI. Taken together, neuroscience and empathic AI demonstrate the way in which psychosomatic human persons as the *imago Dei* mirror the divine archetype in their multi-layered lives.

5 Conclusion

Let us circle back to the epigraph, which indicates that the human creation in the *imago Dei* is tied up with gratitude, while also associated with humility arising from confrontation with humanity's miserable condition. This Element has explored how the holistic interpretation of the *imago Dei* – the psychosomatic human being as the image and ectype of the divine archetype – brings to light both the role of humanity in narrating religious and ethical stories and the condition under which humans would forsake the role and be reluctant to narrate these stories, albeit that it is impossible for them to rule out these narratives altogether. For the *imago Dei* is the ontological basis of being human.

This Element has been dedicated to teasing out the religious and ethical significance of the *imago Dei* in three sections. Section 2 examined the four conventional interpretations of the *imago Dei*: the substantive or the structural, the functional, the relational and the eschatological. They produce four hermeneutical frameworks for spelling out the meaning of being the image of God. None of the four frameworks can be entirely dismissed, as each of them fleshes out a particular aspect of the *imago Dei*. Hence, a holistic account of the *imago Dei* is called for to integrate and go beyond these four hermeneutical approaches.

Section 3 enquired into the holistic account of the *imago Dei* with the aid of the conceptual pair of archetype and ectype. This Reformed thinking offers the conceptual scaffolding of the human being as the ectype of the divine archetype, laying an ontological foundation for understanding the *imago* in the sense of psychosomatic humanity. With this in mind, the *imago Dei* signifies the covenantal stories of God and humans and the stories of ethical performances towards others, on the one hand, and, on the other hand, motivates human persons to narrate these stories throughout the history of humanity. As such, while placing emphasis on the psychosomatic unity of humanity, the holistic account assigns great weight to the collective significance of the *imago Dei*. Furthermore, a considerable amount of space has been devoted to looking into the challenges that atheism may pose to the view of the *imago Dei* as the motivator for narrating God-human stories, ruling out the ostensible contradiction between the theology of the *imago Dei* and atheism. With the aid of the cognitive science of religion, the *imago Dei* has been portrayed as the quintessence of humanity, leading to the corollary that all humans – including atheists – are disposed towards narrating religious and ethical stories.

Section 4 illustrated how the psychosomatic human person narrates religious and ethical stories through engagement with neuroscience and AI. Neurotheology suggests that the human being is created with biological capacities to sense the divine. The *imago Dei* signifies God-human stories, and humans are *biologically* motivated to narrate these religious stories. Exploring empathic AI proves that the narration of ethical stories through empathic action is requisite for humanity. Being human means behaving in an empathic manner towards others. As the *imago Dei*, humans utilise empathic AI not as a replacement for human–human relationships but as an assistant to augment their capability to narrate the stories of ethical performances towards others. These two case studies demonstrate that the religious and ethical implications of the holistic account of the *imago Dei* extend beyond the context of the Christian faith and permeate our quotidian life.

Be that as it may, the profound significance of the holistic interpretation of the *imago Dei* merits further investigation. A case in point is how the psychosomatic human being as the *imago Dei* may assist in fostering the narration of God-human stories within a particular cultural context. Given that the *imago Dei* implies human existence within particular communities, each human person should narrate God-human stories within the parameters of their received culture. As such, the holistic account of the *imago Dei* entails inter-cultural and cross-cultural dialogue on the narration of God-human stories, ensuring the contextual characteristics of Christian theological reflection while preserving the universal God-human story that has been unfolding since Genesis 2.

A second example is concerning how the holistic interpretation of the *imago Dei* may benefit the interaction between theological anthropology and the construal of humanity in other cultures. For instance, I (Xu 2017, 298–324) have comparatively investigated the theological theme of the *imago Dei* and modern new Confucian Mou Zongsan's philosophical view of humanity.

I suggest that the *imago Dei* is resonant with Mou's heavenly decree, which refers to an imperishable and transcendent standard that is immanentised within the human being and guides human moral life. As the Chinese cultural equivalent for the *imago Dei*, the philosophy of the heavenly decree is conducive to shedding light on how the theological stories of ethical performances towards others may be narrated within Chinese communities. Further enquiry would be required to probe how the holistic account of the *imago Dei* finds an echo in the meaning of being human in other cultures.

The theological theme of the *imago Dei* is the basis of Christian anthropology by virtue of the rationale that the *imago Dei per se* is the ontological underpinning of humanity. The *imago* reveals human dignity and uniqueness and enables humans to grapple with the frailty of the human condition and to exhibit their religious and ethical uniqueness in their quotidian life and pilgrimage to the given future. With gratitude and humility, the psychosomatic human person as the *imago Dei* mirrors the divine archetype.

References

Alogna, Victoria K., Jesse Bering, Evan Balkcom, and Jamin Halberstadt. 2019. 'Religious Intuitions and the Nature of "Belief"'. *Studia Humana* 8 (3): 58–68.

Antinoff, Steve. 2009. *Spiritual Atheism*. Berkeley, CA: Counterpoint.

Aquinas, Thomas. 2012. *Summa Theologiae*. Translated by Fr. Laurence Shapcote. *Latin/English Edition of the Works of St. Thomas Aquinas*, 13–20 vols., edited by The Aquinas Institute. Green Bay, WI: Aquinas Institute.

Ashbrook, James B. 1984. 'Neurotheology: The Working Brain and the Work of Theology'. *Zygon: Journal of Religion & Science* 19 (3): 331–350.

———. 1996. 'Making Sense of God: How I Got to the Brain'. *Zygon: Journal of Religion & Science* 31 (3): 401–420.

Augustine. 1963. *The Trinity*. Translated by Stephen McKenna. *The Fathers of the Church*, vol. 45, edited by Hermigild Dressler. Washington: The Catholic University of America Press.

———. 2002. 'The Literal Meaning of Genesis'. In *On Genesis*, edited by John E. Rotelle, In Works of Saint Augustine, vol. I/13, 155–506. New York: New City Press.

Bainbridge, William Sims. 2010. 'Cognitive Science and the New Atheism'. In *Religion and the New Atheism: A Critical Appraisal*, edited by Amarnath Amarasingam. 79–93. Leiden: Brill.

Barbour, Ian G. 1993. *Ethics in an Age of Technology: The Gifford Lectures 1989–1991*, vol. 2. New York: HarperSanFrancisco.

Barr, James. 1968. 'The Image of God in the Book of Genesis – A Study of Terminology'. *Bulletin of the John Rylands Library* 51: 11–26.

———. 1993. *Biblical Faith and Natural Theology*. Oxford: Clarendon Press.

Barrett, Justin L. 2004. *Why Would Anyone Believe in God?* Lanham, MD: Altamira.

———. 2010. 'The Relative Unnaturalness of Atheism: On Why Geertz and Markússon Are Both Right and Wrong'. *Religion* 40: 169–172.

———. 2011. *Cognitive Science, Religion, and Theology*. West Conshohocken, PA: Templeton Press.

Barrett, Justin L., and Tyler S. Greenway. 2017. '*Imago Dei* and Animal Domestication: Cognitive-Evolutionary Perspectives on Human Uniqueness and the *Imago Dei*'. In *Human Origins and the Image of God: Essays in*

Honor of J. Wentzel van Huyssteen, edited by Christopher Lilley and Daniel J. Pedersen, 64–81. Grand Rapids, MI: Eerdmans.

Barrett, Justin L., and Jonathan A. Lanman. 2008. 'The Science of Religious Beliefs'. *Religion* 38: 109–124.

Barrett, Justin L., and Roger Trigg. 2014. 'Cognitive and Evolutionary Studies of Religion'. In *The Roots of Religion: Exploring the Cognitive Science of Religion*, edited by Roger Trigg and Justin L. Barrett, 1–15. London: Routledge.

Barth, Karl. 2004. *Church Dogmatics*. 5 vols., edited by Geoffrey W. Bromiley and Thomas F. Torrance. London: T&T Clark.

Bauckham, Richard. 2010. *Bible and Ecology: Rediscovering the Community of Creation*. London: Darton, Longman and Todd.

Bavinck, Herman. 2004. *Reformed Dogmatics, Volume 2: God and Creation*. Translated by John Vriend, edited by John Bolt. Grand Rapids, MI: Baker.

2006. *Reformed Dogmatics, Volume 3: Sin and Salvation in Christ*. Translated by John Vriend, edited by John Bolt. Grand Rapids, MI: Baker.

Beauregard, Mario. 2024. 'Neuroimaging and Spiritual Practice'. In *The Oxford Handbook of Psychology and Spirituality*, edited by Lisa J. Miller, 632–653. Oxford: Oxford University Press.

Beauregard, Mario, and Denyse O'Leary. 2007. *The Spiritual Brain: A Neuroscientist's Case for the Existence of the Soul*. Portland, ME: HarperOne.

Beauregard, Mario, and Vincent Paquette. 2006. 'Neural Correlates of a Mystical Experience in Carmelite Nuns'. *Neuroscience Letters* 405 (3): 186–190.

Bering, Jesse. 2002. 'Intuitive Conceptions of Dead Agents' Minds: The Natural Foundations of Afterlife Beliefs as Phenomenological Boundary'. *Journal of Cognition and Culture* 2 (4): 263–308.

Berkouwer, Gerrit Cornelis 1962. *Man: The Image of God*. Translated by Dirk W. Jellema. Grand Rapids, MI: Eerdmans.

Berry, Robert James 2012. 'Biology since Darwin'. In *Darwinism and Natural Theology*, edited by Andrew Robinson. 12–38. Newcastle: Cambridge Scholars.

Bimson, John J. 2009. 'Doctrines of the Fall and Sin after Darwin'. In *Theology after Darwin*, edited by Michael Northcott and Robert James Berry. 106–122. Milton Keynes: Paternoster.

Blenkinsopp, Joseph. 2011. *Creation, Un-Creation, Re-Creation: A Discursive Commentary on Genesis 1–11*. London: T&T Clark.

Boyer, Pascal. 2022. 'The Cognitive Study of Religious Activity: Beyond Religion and Belief'. In *The Oxford Handbook of the Cognitive Science of Religion*, edited by Justin L. Barrett, 48–64. Oxford: Oxford University Press.

Braaten, Carl E., and LaVonne Braaten. 1976. *The Living Temple: A Practical Theology of the Body and the Foods of the Earth*. Eugene, OR: Wipf & Stock.

Braddock, Matthew. 2018. 'An Evidential Argument for Theism from the Cognitive Science of Religion'. In *New Developments in the Cognitive Science of Religion: The Rationality of Religious Belief*, edited by Hans van Eyghen, Rik Peels, and Gijsbert van den Brink. 171–198. Cham: Springer.

Briggs, Richard S. 2010. 'Humans in the Image of God and Other Things Genesis Does Not Make Clear.' *Journal of Theological Interpretation* 4 (1–2): 111–126.

Brink, David O. 2007. 'The Autonomy of Ethics'. In *The Cambridge Companion to Atheism*, edited by Michael Martin, 149–165. Cambridge: Cambridge University Press.

Brueggemann, Walter. 2005. *Theology of the Old Testament: Testimony, Dispute, Advocacy*. Minneapolis, MN: Fortress.

Burdett, Michael. 2020. 'Niche Construction and the Functional Model of the Image of God'. *Philosophy, Theology and the Sciences* 7 (2): 158–180.

Burdett, Michael S. 2015. 'The Image of God and Human Uniqueness: Challenges from the Biological and Information Sciences'. *The Expository Times* 127 (1): 3–10.

Calvin, John. 2011. *Institutes of the Christian Religion, Volume 1 & 2*. Translated by Ford Lewis Battles, edited by John T. McNeill. Louisville, KY: Westminster John Knox Press.

Churchland, Patricia S. 2011. *Braintrust: What Neuroscience Tells Us about Morality*. Princeton, NJ: Princeton University Press.

Clines, David J. A. 1968. 'The Image of God in Man'. *Tyndale Bulletin* 19: 53–103.

Coin, Allen, and Veljko Dubljević. 2021. 'Carebots for Eldercare: Technology, Ethics, and Implications'. In *Trust in Human-Robot Interaction*, edited by Chang S. Nam and Joseph B. Lyons, 553–569. London: Academic Press.

Cortez, Marc. 2010. *Theological Anthropology: A Guide for the Perplexed*. New York: T&T Clark International.

Crisp, Oliver. 2015. 'A Christological Model of the *Imago Dei*'. In *The Ashgate Research Companion to Theological Anthropology*, edited by Joshua Ryan Farris and Charles Taliaferro, 217–229. Farnham: Ashgate.

Davis, Stephen T. 2015. 'Redemption, the Resurrected Body, and Human Nature'. In *The Ashgate Research Companion to Theological*

Anthropology, edited by Joshua Ryan Farris and Charles Taliaferro, 293–302. Farnham: Ashgate.

De Cruz, Helen. 2016. 'The Naturalness of Religious Belief: Epistemological Implications'. In *The Blackwell Companion to Naturalism*, edited by Kelly James Clark, 481–493. Chichester: Wiley Blackwell.

De Cruz, Helen, and Johan De Smedt. 2013. 'Reformed and Evolutionary Epistemology and the Noetic Effects of Sin'. *International Journal for Philosophy of Religion* 74: 49–66.

2015. *A Natural History of Natural Theology: The Cognitive Science of Theology and Philosophy of Religion*. Cambridge, MA: MIT.

De La Mettrie, Julien Offray. 1996. 'Machine Man'. In *Machine Man and Other Writings*, edited by Ann Thomson, 1–40. Cambridge: Cambridge University Press.

De Smedt, Johan, and Helen De Cruz. 2014. 'The Imago Dei as a Work in Progress: A Perspective from Paleoanthropology'. *Zygon: Journal of Religion and Science* 49, 1: 135–156.

Deane-Drummond, Celia E. 2012. 'Response: Homo Divinus–Myth or Reality?' In *Darwinism and Natural Theology: Evolving Perspectives*, edited by Andrew Robinson. 39–46. Cambridge: Cambridge Scholars.

2014. *The Wisdom of the Liminal: Evolution and Other Animals in Human Becoming*. Grand Rapids, MI: Eerdmans.

2017. 'In Adam All Die?: Questions at the Boundary of Niche Construction, Community Evolution, and Original Sin'. In *Evolution and the Fall*, edited by William T. Cavanaugh and James K. A. Smith, 23–47. Grand Rapids, MI: Eerdmans.

Decety, Jean, Inbal Ben-Ami Bartal, Florina Uzefovsky, and Ariel Knafo-Noam. 2016. 'Empathy as a Driver of Prosocial Behaviour: Highly Conserved Neurobehavioural Mechanisms'. *Philosophical Transactions of the Royal Society of London. Series B. Biological Sciences* 371 (1686): 20150077.

Dietrich, Jan. 2023. 'Anthropologies of the Hebrew Bible'. In *T&T Clark Handbook of Anthropology and the Hebrew Bible*, edited by Emanuel Pfoh, 245–262. London: T&T Clark.

Dixon, Sandra, and Charles T. Wilcox. 2016. 'The Counseling Implications of Neurotheology: A Critical Review'. *Journal of Spirituality in Mental Health* 18 (2): 91–107.

Emery, Gilles. 2007. *The Trinitarian Theology of Saint Thomas Aquinas*. Translated by Francesca Aran Murphy. Oxford: Oxford University Press.

Fergusson, David. 2009. *Faith and Its Critics: A Conversation*. text. Oxford: Oxford University Press.

2013. 'Humans Created according to the *Imago Dei*: An Alternative Proposal'. *Zygon: Journal of Religion and Science* 48 (2): 439–453.

2017. 'Are We Alone? and Does It Matter?: The Narrative of Human Particularity'. In *Human Origins and the Image of God: Essays in Honor of J. Wentzel van Huyssteen*, edited by Christopher Lilley and Daniel J. Pedersen, 236–249. Grand Rapids, MI: Eerdmans.

2018. *The Providence of God: A Polyphonic Approach*. Cambridge: Cambridge University Press.

2024. 'Is Religion Natural? Boyle Lecture 2024'. *Zygon: Journal of Religion & Science* 59 (4): 1154–1171.

Foerst, Anne. 1998. 'Cog, a Humanoid Robot, and the Question of the Image of God'. *Zygon: Journal of Religion and Science* 33 (1): 91–111.

Gerhard, Johann. 2009. *On the Nature of Theology and on Scripture*. Translated by Richard J. Dinda, edited by Benjamin T. G. Mayes. Saint Louis: Concordia Publishing House.

Goldingay, John. 2020. *Genesis*. Grand Rapids, MI: Baker Academic.

Gonzalez-Liencres, Cristina, Simone G. Shamay-Tsoory, and Martin Brüne. 2013. 'Towards a Neuroscience of Empathy: Ontogeny, Phylogeny, Brain Mechanisms, Context and Psychopathology'. *Neuroscience and Biobehavioral Reviews* 37: 1537–1548.

Graystone, Andrew. 2021. 'Sextech: Simulated Relationships with Machines'. In *The Robot Will See You Now: Artificial Intelligence and the Christian Faith*, edited by John Wyatt and Stephen N. Williams, 151–165. London: SPCK.

Green, Joel B. 2015. 'Why the *Imago Dei* Should Not Be Identified with the Soul'. In *The Ashgate Research Companion to Theological Anthropology*, edited by Joshua Ryan Farris and Charles Taliaferro, 179–190. Farnham: Ashgate.

Gregory Nazianzen. 1894. 'Select Orations of Saint Gregory Nazianzen'. In *S. Cyril of Jerusalem, S. Gregory Nazianzen*, edited by Philip Schaff and Henry Wace, In Nicene and Post-Nicene Fathers, Second Series, 203–434. New York: Christian Literature Company.

2001. *On God and Man: The Theological Poetry of St Gregory of Nazianzus*. Translated by Peter Gilbert. Crestwood, NY: St Vladimir's Seminary Press.

2003. *Select Orations*. Translated by Martha Vinson. Vol. 107 *The Fathers of the Church*, edited by Thomas P. Halton. Washington, DC: The Catholic University of America Press.

Grenz, Stanley J. 2001. *The Social God and the Relational Self: A Trinitarian Theology of the Imago Dei*. Louisville, KY: Westminster John Knox Press.

Gunton, Colin. 1991. 'Trinity, Ontology and Anthropology: Towards a Renewal of the Doctrine of the *Imago Dei*'. In *Persons, Divine and Human: King's College Essays in Theological Anthropology*, edited by Christoph Schwöbel and Colin E. Gunton, 47–61. Edinburgh: T&T Clark.

Harris, Mark. 2024. 'A Scientist-Theologian's Perspective on Science-Engaged Theology: The Case for "Theology of Science" as a Sub-Discipline within Science and Religion'. In *God and the Book of Nature: Experiments in Theology of Science*, edited by Mark Harris, 13–39. London: Routledge.

Hefner, Philip. 2000. 'Imago Dei: The Possibility and Necessity of the Human Person'. In *The Human Person in Science and Theology*, edited by Niels Henrik Gregersen, Willem B. Drees, and Ulf Görman, 73–94. Edinburgh: T&T Clark.

Hendel, Ronald. 2024. *Genesis 1–11: A New Translation with Introduction and Commentary. The Anchor Yale Bible, IA*. New Haven, CT: Yale University Press.

Heppe, Heinrich. 2007. *Reformed Dogmatics*. Translated by George Thomas Thomson, edited by Ernst Bizer. Eugene, OR: Wipf & Stock.

Herring, Stephen L. 2013. *Divine Substitution: Humanity as the Manifestation of Deity in the Hebrew Bible and the Ancient Near East*. Göttingen: Vandenhoeck & Ruprecht.

Herzfeld, Noreen. 2012. 'In Whose Image? Artificial Intelligence and the Imago Dei'. In *The Blackwell Companion to Science and Christianity*, edited by J. B. Stump and Alan G. Padgett, 500–509. Chichester: Wiley-Blackwell.

Herzfeld, Noreen L. 2002. *In Our Image: Artificial Intelligence and the Human Spirit*. Minneapolis, MN: Fortress.

Hogue, David A. 2006. 'Sensing the Other in Worship: Mirror Neurons and the Empathizing Brain'. *Liturgy* 21 (3): 31–39. http://doi.10.1080/04580630600642742.

Irenaeus. 1885. 'Irenaeus against Heresies'. In *The Apostolic Fathers with Justin Martyr and Irenaeus*, edited by Alexander Roberts and James Donaldson, In The Ante-Nicene Fathers. Buffalo: Christian Literature, 315–567.

Jastrzebski, Andrzej K. 2018. 'The Neuroscience of Spirituality: An Attempt at Critical Analysis'. *Pastoral Psychology* 67: 515–524.

Jeeves, Malcolm. 2017. 'The Testimony of the Spirit: Insights from Psychology and Neuroscience'. In *The Testimony of the Spirit: New Essays*, edited by R. Douglas Geivett and Paul K. Moser, 127–150. Oxford: Oxford University Press.

Jones, Paul Dafydd. 2019. 'Human Being'. In *The Oxford Handbook of Karl Barth*, edited by Paul Dafydd Jones and Paul T. Nimmo, 389–406. Oxford: Oxford University Press.

Junius, Franciscus. 2014. *A Treatise on True Theology: With the Life of Franciscus Junius*. Translated by David C. Noe. Grand Rapids, MI: Reformation Heritage Books.

Kelsey, David H. 2009. *Eccentric Existence: A Theological Anthropology*. 2 vols. Louisville, KY: Westminster John Knox.

Kurian, Nomisha. 2025. 'AI's Empathy Gap: The Risks of Conversational Artificial Intelligence for Young Children's Well-being and Key Ethical Considerations for Early Childhood Education and Care'. *Contemporary Issues in Early Childhood* 26 (1): 132–139.

Lanman, Jonathan A. 2013. 'Atheism and Cognitive Science'. In *The Oxford Handbook of Atheism*, edited by Stephen Bullivant and Michael Ruse, 483–496. Oxford: Oxford University Press.

Levenson, Jon D. 1988. *Creation and the Persistence of Evil: The Jewish Drama of Divine Omnipotence*. Princeton: Princeton University Press.

MacIntyre, Alasdair. 2007. *After Virtue: A Study in Moral Theory*. 3rd ed. Notre Dame, IN: University of Notre Dame Press.

Maibom, Heidi L., ed. 2014. *Empathy and Morality*. Oxford: Oxford University Press.

McCauley, Robert N. 2011. *Why Religion Is Natural and Science Is Not*. Oxford: Oxford University Press.

McFarland, Ian A. 2001. 'When Time Is of the Essence: Aquinas and the *Imago Dei*'. *New Blackfriars* 82 (963): 208–223.

McGilchrist, Iain. 2009. *The Master and His Emissary: The Divided Brain and the Making of the Western World*. New Haven, CT: Yale University Press.

2022. *The Matter with Things: Our Brains, Our Delusions and the Unmaking of the World*. 2 vols. London: Perspectiva.

Messer, Neil. 2017. *Theological Neuroethics: Christian Ethics Meets the Science of the Human Brain*. London: T&T Clark.

Middleton, J. Richard. 2005. *The Liberating Image: The Imago Dei in Genesis 1*. Grand Rapids, MI: Brazos.

Moltmann, Jürgen. 1985. *God in Creation: An Ecological Doctrine of Creation*. London: SCM.

Moritz, Joshua M. 2011. 'Evolution, the End of Human Uniqueness, and the Election of the *Imago Dei*'. *Theology and Science* 9 (3): 307–339.

2020. 'Are Hominins Special? Human Origins as the Image and Likeness of God'. *Theology and Science* 18 (4): 537–551.

Mugg, Joshua, and James T. Turner. 2017. 'Why a Bodily Resurrection?: The Bodily Resurrection and the Mind/Body Relation'. *Journal of Analytic Theology* 5: 121–144.

Muller, Richard A. 2003. *Post-Reformation Reformed Dogmatics, Volume One: Prolegomena to Theology*. 2nd ed. Grand Rapids: Baker.

Newberg, Andrew B. 2010. *Principles of Neurotheology*. Farnham: Ashgate.

Newberg, Andrew B., and Mark Robert Waldman. 2009. *How God Changes Your Brain: Breakthrough Findings from a Leading Neuroscientist*. New York: Ballantine Books.

Newberg, Andrew B., Michael Pourdehnad, Abass Alavi, and Eugene G. D'Aquili. 2003. 'Cerebral Blood Flow during Meditative Prayer: Preliminary Findings and Methodological Issues'. *Perceptual and Motor Skills* 97 (2): 625–630.

Noort, Ed. 2016. 'Taken from the Soil, Gifted with the Breath of Life: The Anthropology of Gen 2:7 in Context'. In *Dust of the Ground and Breath of Life (Gen 2:7): The Problem of a Dualistic Anthropology in Early Judaism and Christianity*, edited by Jacques T. A. G. M. van Ruiten and George H. Van Kooten, 1–15. Leiden: Brill.

Pannenberg, Wolfhart. 1985. *Anthropology in Theological Perspective*. London: T&T Clark.

  1991. *Systematic Theology*, vol. 2. Translated by Geoffrey William Bromiley. Grand Rapids, MI: Eerdmans.

Pasnau, Robert. 2004. *Thomas Aquinas on Human Nature: A Philosophical Study of Summa theologiae Ia 75–89*. Cambridge: Cambridge University Press.

Paul, John, II. 1988. *Apostolic Letter, Mulieris Dignitatem*. Vatican City: Libreria Editrice Vaticana.

Peels, Rik, Hans van Eyghen, and Gijsbert van den Brink. 2018. 'Cognitive Science of Religion and the Cognitive Consequences of Sin'. In *New Developments in the Cognitive Science of Religion: The Rationality of Religious Belief*, edited by Hans van Eyghen, Rik Peels, and Gijsbert van den Brink, 199–214. Cham: Springer.

Pelau, Corina, Dan-Cristian Dabija, and Erina Ene. 2021. 'What Makes an AI Device Human-like? The Role of Interaction Quality, Empathy and Perceived Psychological Anthropomorphic Characteristics in the Acceptance of Artificial Intelligence in the Service Industry'. *Computers in Human Behavior* 122: 106855.

Perry, John, and Joanna Leidenhag. 2021. 'What Is Science-Engaged Theology?' *Modern Theology* 37 (2): 245–253.

Polkinghorne, John. 1994. *Science and Christian Belief: Theological Reflections of a Bottom-Up Thinker*. London: SPCK.

Polkinghorne, John C. 2010. *Encountering Scripture: A Scientist Explores the Bible*. London: SPCK.

Puddefoot, John C. 1996. *God and the Mind Machine: Computers, Artificial Intelligence, and the Human Soul*. London: SPCK.

Ramachandran, Vilayanur S., and Sandra Blakeslee. 1998. *Phantoms in the Brain: Probing the Mysteries of the Human Mind*. New York: William Morrow.

Rea, Michael. 2018. *The Hiddenness of God*. Oxford: Oxford University Press.

Reich, K. Helmut. 2009. 'A Critical View of Cognitive Science's Attempt to Explain Religion and its Development'. In *The Oxford Handbook of the Sociology of Religion*, edited by Peter B. Clarke, 280–299. Oxford: Oxford University Press.

Reinhardt, Karoline. 2022. 'Trust and Trustworthiness in AI Ethics'. *AI and Ethics* 3: 735–744 https://doi.org/10.1007/s43681-022-00200-5.

Rhonheimer, Martin. 2014. 'Moral Reason, Person and Virtue: The Aristotelian-Thomistic Perspective in the Face of Current Challenges from Neurobiology'. *Journal of Moral Theology* 3 (1): 1–17.

Richert, Rebekah A., and Kirsten A. Lesage. 2022. 'The Nature of Humans'. In *The Oxford Handbook of the Cognitive Science of Religion*, edited by Justin L. Barrett, 90–109. Oxford: Oxford University Press.

Rizzolatti, Giacomo, and Corrado Sinigaglia. 2023. *Mirroring Brains: How We Understanding Others from Inside*. Translated by Frances Anderson. Oxford: Oxford University Press.

Rosenberg, Stanley P., Michael Burdett, Michael Lloyd, and Benno Van den Toren, eds. 2018. *Finding Ourselves after Darwin: Conversations on the Image of God, Original Sin, and the Problem of Evil*. Grand Rapids, MI: Baker Academic.

Safdari, Abootaleb. 2025. 'Toward an Empathy-based Trust in Human-otheroid Relations'. *AI & Society* 40: 3123–3138.

Schellenberg, John L. 1993. *Divine Hiddenness and Human Reason*. Ithaca, NY: Cornell University Press.

— 2015. *The Hiddenness Argument: Philosophy's New Challenge to Belief in God*. Oxford: Oxford University Press.

Schnell, Tatjana, and William J. F. Keenan. 2013. 'The Construction of Atheist Spirituality: A Survey-Based Study'. In *Constructs of Meaning and Religious Transformation: Current Issues in the Psychology of Religion*, edited by Herman Westerink, 101–118. Göttingen: Vandenhoeck & Ruprecht.

Shank, John B. 2019. 'Between Isaac Newton and Enlightenment Newtonianism: The "God Question" in the Eighteenth Century'. In *Scientific without God?: Rethinking the History of Scientific Naturalism*, edited by Peter Harrison and Jon H. Roberts, 77–96. Oxford: Oxford University Press.

Sharkey, Noel, and Amanda Sharkey. 2010. 'Living with Robots: Ethical Tradeoffs in Eldercare'. In *Close Engagements with Artificial Companions: Key Social, Psychological, Ethical and Design Issues*, edited by Yorick Wilks, 245–255. Amsterdam: John Benjamins.

Shults, F. LeRon. 2003. *Reforming Theological Anthropology: After the Philosophical Turn to Relationality*. Grand Rapids, MI: Eerdmans.

Slattery, John P. 2020. 'Introduction'. In *T&T Clark Handbook of Christian Theology and the Modern Sciences*, edited by John P. Slattery, 1–11. London: T&T Clark.

Sonderegger, Katherine. 2015. *Systematic Theology, Volume 1: The Doctrine of God*. Minneapolis, MN: Fortress.

Srinivasan, Ramya, and Beatriz San Miguel González. 2022. 'The Role of Empathy for Artificial Intelligence Accountability'. *Journal of Responsible Technology* 9: 1–7 https://doi.org/10.1016/j.jrt.2021.100021.

Stahl, Bernd Carsten. 2020. *Artificial Intelligence for a Better Future: An Ecosystem Perspective on the Ethics of AI and Emerging Digital Technologies*. Cham: Springer.

Stone, Peter, Rodney Brooks, Erik Brynjolfsson, et al. September 2016. *Artificial Intelligence and Life in 2030: One Hundred Year Study on Artificial Intelligence 2015 Study Panel Report*. Stanford University (Stanford). https://ai100.stanford.edu/sites/g/files/sbiybj18871/files/media/file/ai100report10032016fnl_singles.pdf.

Sutanto, Nathaniel Gray. 2025. *A Sense of the Divine: An Affective Model of General Revelation from the Reformed Tradition*. Cambridge: Cambridge University Press.

Te Velde, Dolf, ed. 2015. *Synopsis of a Purer Theology*, vol. 1. Leiden: Brill.

Thiel, John E. 2011. 'Methodological Choices in Kelsey's *Eccentric Existence*'. *Modern Theology* 27 (1): 1–13.

Thomas, Gabrielle. 2019. *The Image of God in the Theology of Gregory of Nazianzus*. Cambridge: Cambridge University Press.

Torrance, Thomas F. 2001. *Calvin's Doctrine of Man*. Eugene, OR: Wipf & Stock.

Turkle, Sherry. 2010. 'In Good Company? On the Threshold of Robotic Companions'. In *Close Engagements with Artificial Companions: Key*

Social, Psychological, Ethical and Design Issues, edited by Yorick Wilks, 3–10. Amsterdam: John Benjamins.

Turretin, Francis. 1992–1997. *Institutes of Elenctic Theology*. Translated by George Musgrave Giger. 3 vols., edited by James T. Dennison Jr. Phillipsburg, KS: P&R Publishing.

Vainio, Oli-Pekka. 2014. '*Imago Dei* and Human Rationality'. *Zygon: Journal of Religion and Science* 49 (1): 121–134.

Vallor, Shannon. 2015. 'Moral Deskilling and Upskilling in a New Machine Age: Reflections on the Ambiguous Future of Character'. *Philosophy and Technology* 28: 107–124 https://doi.org/10.1007/s13347-014-0156-9.

2016. *Technology and the Virtues: A Philosophical Guide to a Future Worth Wanting*. Oxford: Oxford University Press.

2024. *The AI Mirror: How to Reclaim Our Humanity in an Age of Machine Learning*. Oxford: Oxford University Press.

Van Asselt, Willem J. 2011. 'Scholasticism in the Time of Early Orthodoxy (ca. 1560–1620)'. In *Introduction to Reformed Scholasticism*, Joel R. Beeke and Jay T. Collier (Eds.), 103–131. Grand Rapids, MI: Reformation Heritage Books.

Van Eyghen, Hans. 2016. 'Two Types of "Explaining Away" Arguments in the Cognitive Science of Religion'. *Zygon: Journal of Religion & Science* 51 (4): 966–982.

Van den Brink, Gijsbert. 2011. 'Are We Still Special? Evolution and Human Dignity'. *Neue Zeitschrift für systematische Theologie und Religionsphilosophie* 53 (3): 318–332.

2020. *Reformed Theology and Evolutionary Theory*. Grand Rapids, MI: Eerdmans.

Van Huyssteen, J. Wentzel. 2006. *Alone in the World? Human Uniqueness in Science and Theology*. Grand Rapids, MI: Eerdmans.

Visala, Aku. 2014. '*Imago Dei*, Dualism, and Evolution: A Philosophical Defense of the Structural Image of God'. *Zygon: Journal of Religion and Science* 49 (1): 101–120.

2015a. 'Cognition, Brain, and Religious Experience: A Critical Analysis'. In *Handbook of Neuroethics*, edited by Jens Clausen and Neil Levy, 1553–1568. Dordrecht: Springer.

2015b. 'Theological Anthropology and the Cognitive Sciences'. In *The Ashgate Research Companion to Theological Anthropology*, edited by Joshua Ryan Farris and Charles Taliaferro, 57–71. Farnham: Ashgate.

2018. 'Will the Structural Theory of the Image of God Survive Evolution?' In *Finding Ourselves after Darwin: Conversations on the Image of God, Original Sin, and the Problem of Evil*, edited by Stanley P. Rosenberg,

Michael Burdett, Michael Lloyd, and Benno Van den Toren, 64–78. Grand Rapids: Baker Academic.

Visala, Aku, and Agustín Fuentes. 2015. 'Human Nature(s): Human Nature at the Crossroad of Conflicting Interests'. *Theology and Science* 13 (1): 25–42.

von Rad, Gerhard. 1973. *Genesis: A Commentary*. Translated by John H. Marks. Revised ed. Hardcopy. Philadelphia: Westminster.

Vozna, Alina, and Stefania Costantini. 2025. 'Ethical, Legal, and Societal Dimensions of AI-Driven Social Robots in Elderly Healthcare'. *Intelligenza Artificiale* 19 (1): 30–40.

Walters, Kerry. 2010. *Atheism: A Guide for the Perplexed*. New York: Continuum.

Walton, John H. 2006. *Ancient Near Eastern Thought and the Old Testament: Introducing the Conceptual World of the Hebrew Bible*. Grand Rapids, MI: Baker Academic.

Welker, Michael. 2021. *In God's Image: An Anthropology of the Spirit*. Grand Rapids, MI: Eerdmans.

Wenham, Gordon J. 1987. *Genesis 1–15. Vol. 1. Dallas: Word, Incorporated, 1987. Word Biblical Commentary*, vol. 1. Dallas, TX: Word Books.

Westermann, Claus. 1994. *Genesis 1–11: A Continental Commentary*. Minneapolis, MN: Fortress.

White, Claire. 2018. 'What Does the Cognitive Science of Religion Explain?' In *New Developments in the Cognitive Science of Religion: The Rationality of Religious Belief*, edited by Hans van Eyghen, Rik Peels, and Gijsbert van den Brink, 35–49. Cham: Springer.

Wilks, Yorick, ed. 2010. *Close Engagements with Artificial Companions: Key Social, Psychological, Ethical and Design Issues*. Amsterdam: John Benjamins.

Willard, Aiyana K., and Ara Norenzayan. 2013. 'Cognitive Biases Explain Religious Belief, Paranormal Belief, and Belief in Life's Purpose'. *Cognition* 129: 379–391.

Wong, Kam Ming. 2008. *Wolfhart Pannenberg on Human Destiny. Ashgate new critical thinking in religion, theology, and biblical studies*. Aldershot: Ashgate.

Xu, Ximian. 2017. 'The Dialogue between Herman Bavinck and Mou Zongsan on Human Nature and Its Quality'. *Journal of Reformed Theology* 11 (3): 298–324.

2023a. 'Human Sustainability in the Age of Technology: A Theological Proposal on Technomoral Human Futures'. In *Issues in Science and*

Theology: Global Sustainability, edited by Michael Fuller, Mark Harris, Joanna Leidenhag, and Anne Runehov, 187–196. Cham: Springer.

2023b. 'A Theological Account of Artificial Moral Agency'. *Studies in Christian Ethics* 36 (3): 642–659.

2024. *The Digitalised Image of God: Artificial Intelligence, Liturgy, and Ethics*. London: Routledge.

2025. 'Hope, Christian Morality, and the Ethics of Predictive AI'. *Studies in Christian Ethics* 38 (2): 183–200.

Yaden, David B., and Andrew B. Newberg. 2022. *The Varieties of Spiritual Experience: 21st Century Research and Perspectives*. Oxford: Oxford University Press.

Zimmerman, Dean. 1999. 'The Compatibility of Materialism and Survival: The "Falling Elevator" Model'. *Faith and Philosophy: Journal of the Society of Christian Philosophers* 16 (2): 194–212.

Cambridge Elements

Christian Doctrine

Rachel Muers
University of Edinburgh

Rachel Muers is Professor of Divinity at the University of Edinburgh. Her publications include *Keeping God's Silence* (2004), *Living for the Future* (2008), and *Testimony: Quakerism and Theological Ethics* (2015). She is co-editor of *Ford's The Modern Theologians: An Introduction to Christian Theology Since 1918*, 4th edition (2024). She is a former president of the Society for the Study of Theology.

Ashley Cocksworth
University of Roehampton

Ashley Cocksworth is Reader in Theology and Practice at the University of Roehampton, UK. He is the author of *Karl Barth on Prayer*; *Prayer: A Guide for the Perplexed*; and (with David F. Ford) *Glorification and the Life of Faith*. His edited volumes include *T&T Clark Handbook of Christian Prayer*; *Karl Barth: Spiritual Writings*; and (with Rachel Muers), *Ford's The Modern Theologians: An Introduction to Christian Theology since 1918*.

Simeon Zahl
University of Cambridge

Simeon Zahl is Professor of Christian Theology at the University of Cambridge and a Fellow of Jesus College.

About the Series

Elements in Christian Doctrine brings creative and constructive thinking in the field of Christian doctrine to a global audience within and beyond the academy. The series demonstrates the vitality of Christian doctrine and its capacity to engage with contemporary questions.

Cambridge Elements⹄

Christian Doctrine

Elements in the Series

Life after Death after Marx
Simon Hewitt

A Theology of Home in a Time of Homelessness
Siobhán Garrigan

*A Sense of the Divine: An Affective Model of General Revelation
from the Reformed Tradition*
N. Gray Sutanto

A Theology of Becoming: Body, Blood, Birth, and Sacrament
Tina Beattie

The *Imago Dei: A Holistic Account*
Ximian Xu

A full series listing is available at: www.cambridge.org/ECDR

For EU product safety concerns, contact us at Calle de José Abascal, 56–1°, 28003 Madrid, Spain or eugpsr@cambridge.org.